Constitutional Amendments

Constitutional Amendments

From Freedom of Speech to Flag Burning

Volume 1:
Amendments 1–8

Tom Pendergast, Sara Pendergast, and John Sousanis
Elizabeth Shaw Grunow, Editor

AN IMPRINT OF THE GALE GROUP

DETROIT · NEW YORK · SAN FRANCISCO
LONDON · BOSTON · WOODBRIDGE, C

Constitutional Amendments
From Freedom of Speech to Flag Burning

Tom Pendergast
Sara Pendergast
John Sousanis

Staff

Elizabeth Shaw Grunow, U·X·L Editor
Carol DeKane Nagel, U·X·L Managing Editor
Thomas L. Romig, U·X·L Publisher

Elizabeth Des Chenes, Richard Clay Hanes, Kris E. Palmer, Contributing Editors

Julie Juengling, Permissions Associate (Pictures)
Robyn Young, Imaging and Multimedia Content Editor
Pamela A. Reed, Imaging Coordinator

Rita Wimberley, Senior Buyer
Evi Seoud, Assistant Manager, Composition Purchasing and Electronic Prepress

Kenn Zorn, Senior Art Director
Pamela A. E. Galbreath, Senior Art Designer

Linda Mahoney, LM Design, Typesetting

Cover photographs: Reproduced by permission of the Library of Congress.

Library of Congress Cataloging-in-Publication Data
Pendergast, Tom.
  Constitutional amendments from freedom of speech to flag burning / Tom Pendergast,
  Sara Pendergast, and John Sousanis ; Elizabeth Shaw Grunow, editor.
    p. cm.
  Includes bibliographical references and index.
  ISBN 0-7876-4865-5 (set: hardcover)-ISBN 0-7876-4866-3 (v.1)-ISBN 0-7876-4867-1
  (v.2)-ISBN 0-7876-4868-X (v.3)
    1.Constitutional amendments-United States-Juvenile literature. 2. Constitutional
  law-United States-Juvenile literature. 3. Civil rights-United States-Juvenile literature.
  [1. Constitutional amendments. 2. Constitutional law. 3. Civil rights.] I. Title:
  Constitutional amendments. II. Pendergast, Sara. III. Sousanis, John. IV. Title.

  KF4557 .P46 2001
  342.73'03-dc21

                                                                          00-067236

Contents

Volume 1

Contents

Volume Two

Volume Three

Contents

Reader's Guide

The Constitution of the United States has been the supreme law of the land for more than two centuries, since it was formally adopted in 1788. The Constitution's longevity as the basis for the U.S. government owes much to its original framers. Their decision to provide a system of checks and balances among the various branches of government and to create a form of representation that took into account the interests of big and small states left room for a growing country to adapt and reinterpret the Constitution. However, the Constitution has never been a purely static document: because the framers created a process for amending the Constitution, over the years the document has been changed and expanded in response to changes in American society. It is a process that is never taken lightly, for it means tinkering with the very framework of the nation's political system. Yet from the years immediately following its ratification through the 1990s, Americans have successfully amended the Constitution twenty-seven times, and made attempts to change it numerous other times.

Constitutional Amendments: From Freedom of Speech to Flag Burning devotes a single chapter to each of the existing amendments to the United States Constitution as well as a final chapter that looks at several amendment proposals that have not been ratified.

An Introduction provides general information about the drafting of the Constitution, the interpretive powers of the Supreme Court, and the ratification process that supplements the information provided for each of the individual amendments.

Chapters average approximately six thousand words in length and examine the historical origins of the amendment, the drafting and ratifi-

Reader's Guide

cation of the amendment, and the consequent impact the amendment has had on American society. In general, cases pertaining to an amendment are discussed in chronological order. However, in some instances an amendment's various clauses are discussed separately in order to clarify the particular significance of each clause.

Additional Features

Constitutional Amendments is organized for easy fact-finding:

- Each chapter is headed by the full text of the constitutional amendment it is covering.

- Standard sidebars containing the ratification facts of each amendment also appear at the beginning of each chapter.

- The issues and amendments are presented in language accessible to middle school users.

- Challenging terms are sometimes used, so a Words to Know section is included in each volume. The section defines words and terms used in the set that may be unfamiliar to students.

- Sources for further study are included at the end of each chapter.

- The three volumes also contain more than 150 photos and illustrations to further enhance the text.

- Each of the three volumes also includes a research topics section and a general subject index for locating key people, places, events, and cases discussed throughout *Constitutional Amendments*.

Suggestions Are Welcome

We welcome your comments on *Constitutional Amendments: From Freedom of Speech to Flag Burning.* Please write, Editors, *Constitutional Amendments,* U•X•L, 27500 Drake Road, Farmington Hills, MI 48331-3535; call toll-free: 1-800-877-4253; fax to 248-414-5043; or send e-mail via http://www.galegroup.com.

Advisory Board

Special thanks are due for the invaluable comments and suggestions provided by U•X•L's *Constitutional Amendments advisors:*

- Connie Altimore, American History teacher, Northeast Middle School, Midland, Michigan
- Nancy Guidry, Young Adult Librarian, Santa Monica Public Library, Santa Monica, California
- Ann Marie LaPrise, Children's Librarian and Assistant Manager, Elmwood Park Branch, Detroit Public Library, Detroit, Michigan

Contributors

The following writers contributed to U•X•L's *Constitutional Amendments:*

- John Sousanis, chapters 1-10, 12
- Tina Gianoulis, chapters 11, 16, 24, 27
- Richard Clay Hanes, chapters 13-15
- Sara Pendergast, chapters 17, 25
- Tom Pendergast, chapters 18, 21, 22, 23 (with Tim Seul), 28
- Tim Seul, chapters 19, 20, 23 (with Tom Pendergast), 26

Research and Activity Ideas

The following list of research and activity ideas is intended to offer suggestions for complementing social studies and history curricula, to trigger additional ideas for enhancing learning, and to suggest cross-disciplinary projects for library and classroom use.

Discussing a Free Press: The First Amendment limits government interference with a free press. Consider how the news media might differ if the government were allowed to directly influence or censor the press. Make a list of all the stories in a single edition of a newspaper or weekly news magazine. Have students discuss which stories might be censored if the First Amendment didn't exist. Physically cut these stories from the publication to demonstrate the impact the Amendment has had. For further discussion, have students suggest stories that a government-controlled press might add to a newspaper, such as articles praising officials or government actions. Finally, discuss the impact a government-controlled press might have on today's society.

Religious Diversity: The First Amendment's Establishment Clause helps protect religious diversity in the United States. Using almanacs, census data, or other sources, create graphs and charts that compare how many different religions are practiced in your community, your county, and your state. Discuss how life might be different if there were a single government-established religion.

Debating the Right to Bear Arms: Over the years the Second Amendment has been interpreted quite differently by different groups. Groups debate whether the amendment simply protects a

**Research
and Activity
Ideas**

state's right to establish a militia or whether it also guarantees the individual's right to own weapons. After discussing the chapter on the Second Amendment divide the class in half, with each half taking one side of the debate. The students in each group should work together to rewrite the amendment in a way they believe clearly states their side of the debate. Then have the entire class discuss how the proposed amendments would affect today's society.

Living the Third Amendment: The Third Amendment limits the practice of quartering (or housing) soldiers in private homes. During the French and Indian War, American colonist were sometimes forced to house British soldiers in their homes. Imagine that your family has been asked to house one or more soldiers. Write a journal entry discussing how such an arrangement might impact your daily life.

Voting Rights: The Fifteenth, Nineteenth and Twenty-sixth Amendments granted the right to vote to groups of people who were previously denied the right. To help students understand the importance of political participation, divide the class into groups by gender, birth months, or other criteria. Then put several fictitious decisions up for a vote, such as which popular band the class would like to invite to play at the school or which team sport should be cut from the school's athletic program. With each vote, look at how the results would differ if one or another group's votes were not counted. Discuss the impact of limiting or widening the number of people allowed to vote in real elections.

Government Bans: Look at the history of the temperance (anti-alcohol) movement. Discuss why the Eighteenth Amendment prohibition on alcohol sales and consumption was passed and the reasons the Twenty-first Amendment later repealed it. Consider the difficulties of establishing a complete ban on other products considered unhealthy or dangerous, such as cigarettes.

Interpreting Amendments: Over the years the Supreme Court has changed the way it interprets various Constitutional amendments. Track the Court's changing interpretation of a particular amendment from the time it was passed to the present day. Discuss how the same amendment could be understood differently at different times in history and by different justices.

Draft a New Amendment: Divide your class into groups and have each group choose an issue they feel strongly about. Have the group write a proposal for a constitutional amendment that incorporates their idea. Issues could range from serious political issues to more frivolous ideas such as imposing a national dress code. Each group should then present its amendment for debate with the rest of the class. Discuss whether the amendments might be interpreted to mean something other than what the drafters intended. After the class discussion, allow each group to rewrite their amendment. Finally, put the redrafted amendments up for a vote of the class.

Unratified Amendments: Chapter twenty-eight looks at a number of unratified constitutional amendments. Have students write an essay on how American society might be different if one of these amendments were ratified.

Words to Know

A

Abolition: Total opposition to all slavery.

Abolitionists: Those who fought for an end to slavery.

Abortion: A biological event or medical procedure that terminates a pregnancy.

Abridge: To lessen.

Absentee ballot: A ballot that can be mailed in, so that a person can vote if they are away from home during an election.

Abstinence: The act of abstaining or avoiding something, for instance, the use of alcoholic beverages.

Acquittal: A trial outcome in which a defendant is free from a charge.

Activist: Someone who works hard for a political cause.

Aerial surveillance: Watching activity from the air, usually in a helicopter or airplane.

Affirmation: A solemn declaration.

Appeal: A legal proceeding in which a case is taken before a higher court for rehearing.

Apportionment: The process of determining how many representatives a particular state, county, or other kind of region should send to a legislature.

Articles of Confederation: An early constitution for the United States that set up a weak central government. The document was ratified in 1781 but was replaced by the U.S. Constitution in 1789.

Assistance of counsel: The help of outsiders in a trial. The term usually applies to the aid of a professional attorney.

Attorney: A person who is legally qualified to represent someone or some group in a court of law. A lawyer.

B

Billet: Lodging for troops in nonmilitary buildings.

Bill of Rights: The first ten amendments to the U.S. Constitution. These amendments clarify certain personal freedoms not clearly defined in the language of the Constitution.

Bipartisan: Supported by two groups/political parties.

Bond: A certificate issued by a company or government that promises to pay back the cost of the certificate with interest.

Bootlegging: The illegal manufacture, sale, or transportation of liquor.

Bounty: A reward for performing a certain task.

Boycott: A political tactic by which a group of people refuse to use a product or service to protest something they don't like about the producers of the product or service.

British Empire: Worldwide territories governed by or linked to Great Britain.

C

Candidate: A person nominated for a political office.

Capital crime: A crime that is punishable by death.

Capital gains: The profit that is made from selling something.

Civil rights: A series of basic rights written in the Constitution and identified through time that are to be enjoyed by all citizens without undue government interference.

Civil trial: A trial in which a person (or group) who has been injured seeks payment from the person who caused the injury. In a civil trial the person bringing the case to the court is seeking a remedy (solution) to a problem, whereas in a criminal trial an entity (usually the state) is seeking to have someone punished for an illegal action.

Civil War: War fought between the Northern (Union) states and the Southern (Confederate) states from 1861 to1865 over issues such as state and federal power and the future of slavery in the United States.

Coalition: A temporary alliance of different groups seeking a similar goal.

Cold War: A state of political tension between the Soviet Union and the United States that lasted from roughly 1947 to 1989.

Colony: A territory controlled by a distant government.

Commerce: The large-scale exchange of goods and products involving transportation.

Common law: Legal tradition. Many of America's legal traditions can be traced to English common law.

Compensation: Something given to someone in return for something else; often, payment given in exchange for work performed.

Compromise of 1850: A political deal aimed at easing the conflict between slave and free states, this compromise allowed California to join the United States as a free state in exchange for giving slave owners the right to travel into free territory to capture runaway slaves.

Compulsory process: A process by which courts subpoena (command someone to appear in court) witnesses for the defense and prosecution.

Confederacy: Also known as the Confederate States of America; the eleven Southern states that seceded, or withdrew, from the United States during the Civil War (1861–65).

Congress: The legislative, or law making, branch of the U.S. government. Congress is made up of two parts, called houses: the Senate and the House of Representatives. The Senate gives each state equal representation, while representation in the House of Representatives is roughly proportionate to the state's share of the country's total population.

Words to Know

Conscription: Compulsory enrollment in the armed forces; the draft.

Consensus: Widespread agreement; an opinion reached by the majority.

Construe: To interpret.

Consumer: Someone who uses or buys a product or service.

Conviction: A trial outcome in which a defendant is found guilty of a charge.

Corruption: Wrong-doing in government.

Criminal trial: A trial in which the government seeks to punish someone for a crime. In a criminal trial an entity (usually the state) is seeking to have someone punished for an illegal action, whereas in a civil trial the person bringing the case to the court is seeking a remedy (solution) to a problem.

D

Declaration of Independence: Completed on July 4, 1776, the document—which was written primarily by Thomas Jefferson—lists the complaints of the thirteen American colonies against Great Britain and formally announces their independence from the British Empire.

Deduction: In taxes, an expense a taxpayer can subtract from his/her taxable income.

Desecration: The violation of something sacred.

Discrimination: Giving privileges to one group but not to another similar group.

Diplomat: Someone who represents the government of his or her country during relations with other countries.

Direct election: An election in which people vote, not an election in which representatives vote in the place of the public.

Domestic product: Something that is made within a country. The opposite of domestic is foreign.

Due process: Proceedings carried out within established guidelines that do not limit or violate a person's legal rights.

E

Effective counsel: Helpful legal assistance.

Electors: Representatives from each state who cast the actual votes for president and vice president of the United States.

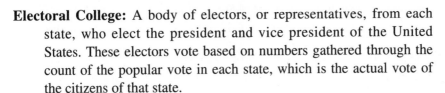

Electoral College: A body of electors, or representatives, from each state, who elect the president and vice president of the United States. These electors vote based on numbers gathered through the count of the popular vote in each state, which is the actual vote of the citizens of that state.

Electoral majority: Votes from a majority of the electors in the Electoral College.

Emancipation: The act of freeing one person from the control and authority of another.

Embargo: A government order forbidding trade with another country.

Eminent domain: Literally, the term means "highest claim to ownership of land." The concept allows a government to take private property for public use because the government is thought to have eminent domain over all the lands it rules.

Enumerated rights: Rights that are specifically defined in the Constitution or its amendments.

Enumeration: An official count, as of the number of citizens in a legislative district.

E pluribus unum: A Latin phrase meaning "Out of many, one." It is one of the mottoes of the United States.

Equal protection of the laws: A right that states that no person or class of persons can be denied the same protection of the laws pertaining to their lives, property, and pursuit of happiness as others in similar circumstances.

Equitable claim: A civil claim in which the plaintiff (person bringing suit in court) seeks to cause the defendant to perform certain actions (or to stop performing others). Equitable claims are not covered by the Seventh Amendment.

Ethics: Moral values.

Words to Know

Evangelical: Characterized by ardent or crusading enthusiasm. Evangelical churches actively seek to spread their message and recruit new members.

Exclusionary rule: A legal concept asserting that evidence found during an illegal search should not be used against a defendant in court. The exclusionary rule is a relatively recent concept in legal history that is now applied in most American criminal trials.

Excise tax: An extra charge added to the price of some domestic products.

Exemption: In taxes, part of the income on which the taxpayer is allowed not to pay taxes.

Express powers: Federal powers that are specifically enumerated or listed in the Constitution or its amendments.

F

Faithless elector: A term used to describe a representative who does not vote the way he or she had promised to before being selected to the Electoral College. By the end of the twentieth century, only eight electors in the history of the Electoral College had cast such "faithless" votes.

Farmer's alliances: Groups of farmers who met to discuss their problems and agree on common goals so that they could increase their political power and improve the conditions of their lives.

Federalism: The type of government in which separate states come together to form a union. Also, the kind of politics within such a government by which people believe the states should have their own identity and power separate from the national government.

Federalist Party: A political party founded in 1787 that argued for the establishment of a strong federal (central or national) government.

Federation: A government in which separate states unite for greater strength.

Filibuster: An attempt to obstruct the passage of legislation, often with prolonged speechmaking.

Flat tax: A tax with one rate for everyone.

x x i v   *Constitutional Amendments*

Flogging: Very hard beating, usually with a whip or a stick.

Frisk: To search a person by running ones hand over the person's clothes and through his or her pockets.

Fruit from the poisonous tree: A term for evidence that is obtained as a direct result of other illegally obtained evidence. Such "fruit" is often not allowed to be used in court.

G

General warrant: A type of warrant (a document issued by a judge allowing the holder to search the premises) used by British officials until the end of the eighteenth century. A general warrant lacked probable cause and usually did not name specific people or places to be searched.

Good faith exception: A concept that allows illegally gained evidence to be used in court, if the police officer did not willfully break the law in obtaining it. Allows for honest mistakes by law enforcement officials.

Graduated tax: A tax where the rate increases in steps, little by little.

Grand jury: A group of citizens assembled to decide if the government has enough evidence against an accused person to justify holding a trial.

Great Britain: At the time of the American Revolution, Great Britain was a single state made up of England, Wales, and Scotland. Today, Great Britain, or the United Kingdom, also includes Northern Ireland. Great Britain ruled the thirteen American colonies until the American Revolution in 1776.

Great Depression: A worldwide economic collapse that began with the stock market crash of 1929.

Grievance: A complaint about an unjust act.

H

Historical test: The method used to determine which civil cases are entitled to a jury trial under the Seventh Amendment. If a case in federal courts historically would have been entitled to a jury trial under English common law, a jury is used.

House of Representatives: The lower house in Congress. Each state's representation in the house is roughly proportionate to its share of the total population. Every state has at least one representative.

I

Immunity: Exemption (to be excused) from regular legal requirements and penalties.

Impeachment: The process by which an elected official is removed from office.

Implied powers: Federal powers that are only hinted at or suggested by the Constitution.

Inauguration: The ceremony by which newly elected presidents and vice presidents are sworn into office.

Income: Money earned from working, investing, renting, or selling things.

Incriminate: To accuse or blame someone for a crime.

Indictment: A formal charge prepared by the government against a defendant that is agreed to by a grand jury or by a judge in a hearing.

Informant: A person who gives information or tips to law enforcement officers.

Insurrection: Rising up against established authority.

Integration: To bring together or blend; commonly used to describe a mixture of different races of people.

Internal Revenue Code (U.S. Tax Code): The collection of all the laws and rules that concern federal income tax.

Intervene: To come between.

Involuntary servitude: The state in which a person works for another person against his or her will due to force, imprisonment, or coercion, regardless of whether the person is being paid for their labor.

J

Jeopardy: Exposure to danger of death, loss, or injury. The type of danger a defendant is in while on trial for a criminal offense.

Jim Crow: Legally enforced racial segregation, named after a stereotypical black character in a minstrel show.

Jurisdiction: The power and authority to interpret and apply the law. A court has jurisdiction in a district, or defined area.

Just compensation: A fair payment for losses.

L

Lame duck: A name given to an elected official continuing in office during the period between a failed election bid and the inauguration of a successor. "Lame duck" politicians are thought to be ineffective and without power.

Legislature: An official law-making governmental body or assembly.

Literacy test: A test a voter had to pass before being able to vote in an election. The tests were considered controversial because they prevented those who were denied equal access to an education the right to vote.

Lynch: To execute someone without due process of law, often by hanging.

M

Magistrate: A judge or other court official capable of issuing a warrant.

Magna Carta: A document, signed by King John I of England in 1215, outlining personal and political freedoms granted to English citizens.

Majority: More than half of a total.

Mandate: A show of support by voters for their elected representative. A president is thought to have a mandate to enact his proposals when he receives broad popular support.

Maritime: Relating to navigation or commerce on the seas.

Miranda warnings: Standard warnings about rights and responsibilities that are read or spoken to a suspect in police custody before he or she is interrogated. The Supreme Court established the warnings in the case of *Miranda v. Arizona* (1966).

Missouri Compromise: A political deal aimed at easing the conflict between slave and free states, this 1820 compromise drew a line

across lands acquired in the Louisiana Purchase and declared that states admitted south of the line could allow slave holding but that states north of the line must be free.

Muckraking: Journalism that exposes corruption in public life.

N

Narrow interpretation: To greatly limit the meaning of something.

Naturalization: A process in which a person may gain citizenship by meeting certain requirements such as length of residence or act of Congress.

Nationalism: Within a federation, it is the political belief that the national government should be more powerful than the state governments.

Negotiate: To settle disagreements or resolve issues by discussion and mutual agreement.

Nominate: To appoint or propose a candidate for office.

P

Pacifist: Someone who believes that war or violence is the wrong way to settle disputes.

Parliament: Great Britain's legislative (law-making) assembly.

Particularity requirement: One of the conditions a warrant must meet to be deemed legal under the Fourth Amendment. To meet the particularity requirement, the warrant must list the particular people and places to be searched and the specific kinds of evidence that an officer hopes to obtain.

Party: Group of people organized with the purpose of directing government policies.

Patent: An official government grant giving someone the right to be the only one to make a product or perform a process that he or she invented for a certain period of time.

Patent law: Laws dealing with the ownership of new inventions and commercial processes.

Pensions: Regular payments of money other than for salary, such as for retirement or disability.

Peonage: Forcing a person against his or her will to work for another to pay a debt.

Per diem: Latin, meaning "per day;" the rate of payment a person receives per day.

Plaintiff: The party who sues in a civil action; a complainant; the prosecution—that is, a state or the United States representing the people—in a criminal case.

Plain view rule: A rule that allows officers to seize evidence they do not have a warrant for if they come across the evidence legally.

Plurality: In an election among three or more candidates, a number of votes cast for one candidate that is greater than the number cast for any other candidate, but that is still less than half of the total number of votes.

Plutocrat: A wealthy person with the power to influence government. A plutocracy is a government ruled by a wealthy class.

Police power: A recognized general legal authority not specifically mentioned in the U.S. Constitution that states hold to govern their citizens, lands, or natural resources.

Political appointment: A job within the government that is filled by a person chosen by an elected official.

Poll: A survey by which a random group of people are asked their opinions in order to predict how most people feel about a subject. The Gallup Poll is a respected and famous polling company.

Poll taxes: Fees charged to citizens to vote at the voting (polling) place.

Popular majority: More than half of the votes case by the voting public.

Popular vote: In the U.S. presidential election process, the votes cast by the public rather than by the Electoral College.

Precedent: An instance that serves as an example for dealing with similar situations.

President: The highest elected office in U.S. government. The leader of the executive branch of government.

Presidential disability: The inability of the President to function in office.

President Pro Tempore: Senator who presides over the Senate in the absence of the vice president. Also considered the Senate's presiding officer, the president pro tempore is included in the line of succession should the offices of the president and vice president become vacant.

Probable cause: Information that would lead a reasonable person to believe that an officer's request for a warrant is merited.

Procedural due process: The constitutional guarantee that one's liberty and property rights may not be affected unless reasonable notice and an opportunity to be heard in order to present a claim or defense are provided.

Progressive era: A period from roughly 1900 to 1920 during which many Americans supported the improvement of society through changes in government and social policy.

Progressive tax: A tax that is based upon a person's ability to pay; the more a person earns or has, the more he or she pays in tax.

Prohibition: A period from 1920 to 1933 when the Eighteenth Amendment to the Constitution made the manufacture, sale, or transportation of intoxicating liquors within the United States illegal.

Prosecute: To begin civil or criminal legal proceedings.

Prosecutor: The government attorney in a criminal case.

Public rights: Rights created by Congress that were not in existence at the time the Bill of Rights was adopted. These rights are not subject to the traditions of common law.

R

Radical: Extreme. A radical change is a complete change; a person who is a radical advocates complete change of a system.

Ratification: A process in which three-fourths of the states must approve proposed amendments to the Constitution before the amendment can become formally adopted.

Reasonable expectation of privacy: One of the standards used to determine if a warrant is required to gather evidence. If a person has good reason to expect privacy (such as in their home or their car) a warrant is usually required before searching is permitted.

Redcoat: Slang term for British soldiers that refers to their bright red uniform jackets.

Regressive tax: A tax by which everyone is charged the same rate of tax, no matter how much property or income they may have.

Repeal: To revoke or rescind an official act or law. In the United States the repeal movement was directed to revoking the Eighteenth Amendment; it succeeded in 1933 with the passage of the Twenty-first Amendment.

Republic: A form of government in which government officials are elected by voters.

Retroactive: Something that applies to time already past.

Revenue: The income of a government.

S

Scandal: An embarrassing or dishonest action that offends the public and damages someone's reputation.

Secede: To break away from an organization.

Second Great Awakening: A period between roughly 1820 and 1850 when religious enthusiasm swept the country and church attendance grew dramatically.

Segregation: Keeping racial groups from mixing, such as maintaining separate facilities for members of different races or restricting use of facilities to members of one race.

Seizure: The forcible taking of property or other evidence.

Senate: The upper house of Congress. Two senators represent each state equally in the Senate.

Servitude: Owning another person who performs duties.

Silver platter doctrine: A court ruling that allowed federal officials to use illegally gathered evidence if it were presented to them by state law enforcement officials on "a silver platter." The doctrine was eliminated in 1960.

Slavery: The owning of other persons to perform work.

Sobriety: Moderation or abstinence in the consumption of alcoholic beverages.

Sovereign: The government body or person with supreme authority, such as the president, or a king or queen.

Sovereign immunity: The concept under common law by which the government is protected against any lawsuit by its people. Under certain circumstances, the government may choose to waive this right and allow people to take legal action against it or its agents.

Sovereignty: Controlling body of power or government authority.

Speakeasy: Any place in which people may buy or consume illegal alcoholic beverages.

Speaker of the House of Representatives: The U.S. representative selected to lead the House of Representatives.

Spoils system: A system for making appointments to public office based on how well appointees had served the party in power. The spoils system was often used in the nineteenth century.

State government: The government of an individual state. The Tenth Amendment grants state governments all government power that is not granted to the federal government by the Constitution.

Statesman: Someone who is skilled at the business of government or politics.

Subsidy: Money given by the government to help individuals or businesses.

Substantive due process: The concept that there are certain essential rights that no law can take away.

Subpoena: A court order commanding a person to appear in court.

Succession: The order in which designated people assume a title of office (for example, the presidency).

Suffrage: The right to vote at public elections.

Suffragist: Supporters of a woman's right to vote.

Sumptuary laws: Laws that regulate personal behavior on moral or religious grounds. Opponents of the Eighteenth Amendment complained that it was a sumptuary law.

Supreme Court: The highest court in the United States. Considered the final interpreter of American law.

Supreme Court justice: A judge who serves on the Supreme Court.

T

"Take the fifth": A phrase used to indicate that a person is using their Fifth Amendment protection against self-incrimination.

Tariff: An extra charge added onto the price of an imported product.

Tax bracket: A range of income that is taxed at a certain rate.

Tax evasion: Purposely not paying one's income tax.

Teetotaler: Someone who abstains from drinking any alcohol.

Temperance: A philosophy of moderation or abstinence, especially with regard to alcoholic beverages. The Temperance movement in the United States led to the passage of the Eighteenth Amendment, prohibiting the sale or manufacture of alcohol, in 1919.

Tenure: Length of time in a position or office.

Ticket: A list of candidates for nomination or election.

Tithing: Voluntarily giving a percentage of one's income—most often ten percent—usually to a religious group.

U

Unanimous verdict: A verdict to which all members of a jury agree to.

Unenumerated rights: Rights that exist despite the fact that they are not mentioned or listed in the Constitution.

Union: Name given to the states that did not secede, or withdraw, from the United States during the Civil War (1861–65). The term also refers to a group of workers who unite in order to bargain (set wages and working conditions) with their employer.

Unit rule: A rule that gives all of a state's electoral votes to representatives of the party that wins the popular vote in that state.

V

Valid: Having legal authority or force.

Verdict: The formal decision or finding made by a jury concerning the questions submitted to it during a trial. The jury reports the verdict to the court, which generally accepts it.

Vice president: The second highest elected office in U.S. government. The vice president serves as the president of the Senate and also serves as president if the president is unable to do so.

W

Waive: To willingly give up a right, title, or something that is rightfully due to you.

Warrant: A document issued by a judge allowing the holder to search the premises.

Whig Party: A political party of the nineteenth century that was formed to oppose the Democratic Party. The Whigs encouraged the loose interpretation of the Constitution.

Wiretap: Any electronic device that allows eavesdropping on phone conversations.

Writs of assistance: A form of warrant once used by British officials in the American colonies. The general warrant allowed nearly unlimited searches and seizures of property.

Wrong-winner argument: An argument that states that, under certain circumstances, the Electoral College system in the United States could elect a president that was not, in fact, the people's choice.

Introduction: The Constitution and the Amendment Process

The United States Constitution and its twenty-seven amendments comprise the supreme law of the United States of America. Together they create the structure of American government: granting powers to the branches of government while simultaneously imposing strict limits on those powers. Although written more than two centuries ago, the Constitution has proven able to adapt to the changes in American society—while also helping to shape many of those changes. The ratified constitutional amendments altered aspects of the way Americans govern themselves, and most have had a lasting legal and cultural impact.

A New Nation is Born

In the years before the American Revolutionary War (1775–83) the thirteen original states were individual colonies governed by the British government. The men and women who lived in these territories tended to identify themselves as citizens of the individual colonies (such as Virginians or New Yorkers) rather than as part of a larger America.

In the early 1700s, the colonists found themselves increasingly at odds with the British government over issues such as taxation, tariffs, and the increased presence of the British Army in the colonies (see chapter three). There was a growing feeling within the colonies that Great Britain was infringing upon individual liberties (freedoms). Citizens of the various colonies began to band together in opposition to British rule.

Introduction

As political tension grew within the colonies, military tension grew between the colonial militias (bands of citizen soldiers) and British troops. The first battle of the American Revolution broke out in the spring of 1775. On July 4, 1776, the colonies signed the Declaration of Independence, formally calling for an end to the colonies' political connection to Great Britain. After six years of fighting, the colonies' Continental Army won the last battle of the American Revolutionary War in 1781. The superior leadership of General George Washington (1732–1799) led the colonies to their independence. He eventually became the first president of the United States.

Surprisingly enough, after their successful military cooperation, the thirteen states found that they now valued their independence not only from Great Britain, but also from one another.

The Articles of Confederation: A "league of friendship"

Not surprisingly, when the newly liberated states agreed to form a central government under a document known as the Articles of Confederation and Perpetual Union (commonly referred to as the Articles of Confederation), the government they set up had very little power of its own.

The Articles had originally been drafted in 1776, but were revised and approved by representatives of the thirteen colonies in November 1777. The original proposal was supposed to have created a powerful central government, but by the time the articles were ratified (agreed to) by several states in 1781, the document had been changed dramatically.

Under the Articles of Confederation, the federal (central or national) government was "a firm league of friendship" between the states. The Continental Congress, set up by the Articles of Confederation, was made up of a single assembly (or house) in which each state had only one vote. Nine of the thirteen votes were needed to pass any significant laws, and a unanimous vote was required to change the Articles. There also was no president under the Articles of Confederation, and the national courts were given legal power over very few cases.

SHAYS' REBELLION. The government under the Articles of Confederation was too weak to levy and collect taxes and could neither pay the country's debts nor defend the nation's borders. But it was a military uprising led by Massachusetts farmers that called many politicians' attention to the government's limitations. A severe depression (economic downturn) in the 1780s caused hundreds of farmers to lose their homes and land to debt. In what became known as Shays' Rebellion, several hundred farmers in Massachusetts banded together to protest the farmers' plights. Led by Daniel Shays, a former captain in the Continental Army, the farmers took over courthouses in five counties in the summer and fall of 1786.

Then in January 1787, the farmers marched on federal troops in Springfield, Massachusetts. After ten days of fighting, the federal troops put down the rebellion. But the battle convinced many political leaders that America's central government had to be strengthened. Shortly after Shays' Rebellion, the Continental Congress invited delegates from the states to a convention in Philadelphia, Pennsylvania, to revise the Articles of Confederation.

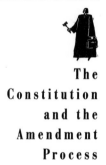

The Philadelphia Convention: Crafting a Stronger Government

The Philadelphia Convention began in May 1787. Interestingly, although the conventioneers were supposed to be working out a plan for strengthening the national government, the convention ended up being divided between Federalists, who favored a stronger central government, and Anti-Federalists, who opposed giving the central government any more power than it already had.

Several prominent Federalists such as James Madison (1751–1836) and Virginia governor Edmund Randolph (1753–1813) were among the first delegates to arrive in Philadelphia. They quickly drafted the so-called "Virginia Plan," which proposed scrapping the Articles of Confederation altogether to create a strong central government consisting of "supreme Legislative, Executive, and Judiciary" branches. The first delegates to attend the convention quickly adopted the Virginia Plan.

As more delegates arrived at the convention, however, the number of Anti-Federalists in attendance grew. The Anti-Federalists believed that the Articles of Confederation needed only a few amendments to make the existing government as effective as it needed to be. The Anti-Federalists plan, known as the "New Jersey Plan," called for giving the central government far less power than the Virginia Plan did.

As each article of the already adopted Virginia Plan was debated at the convention, the Anti-Federalists chipped away at the plan, until the two sides arrived at system of government that represented a compromise between the Federalists and the Anti-Federalists.

Introduction

The Constitution of the United States.

Reproduced by permission of Archive Photos, Inc.

WE the people of the States of of New-Hampshire, Massachusetts, Rhode-Island and Providence Plantations, Connecticut, New-York, New-Jersey, Pennsylvania, Delaware, Maryland, Virginia, North-Carolina, South-Carolina, and Georgia, do ordain, declare and establish the following Constitution for the Government of Ourselves and our Posterity.

ARTICLE I.

The stile of this Government shall be, "The United States of America."

II.

The Government shall consist of supreme legislative, executive and judicial powers.

III.

The legislative power shall be vested in a Congress, to consist of two separate and distinct bodies of men, a House of Representatives, and a Senate; each of which shall, in all cases, have a negative on the other. The Legislature shall meet on the first Monday in December every year.

IV.

Sect. 1. The Members of the House of Representatives shall be chosen every second year, by the people of the several States comprehended within this Union. The qualifications of the electors shall be the same, from time to time, as those of the electors in the several States, of the most numerous branch of their own legislatures.

Sect. 2. Every Member of the House of Representatives shall be of the age of twenty-five years at least; shall have been a citizen in the United States for at least three years before his election; and shall be, at the time of his election, a resident of the State in which he shall be chosen.

Sect. 3. The House of Representatives shall, at its first formation, and until the number of citizens and inhabitants shall be taken in the manner herein after described, consist of sixty-five Members, of whom three shall be chosen in New-Hampshire, eight in Massachusetts, one in Rhode-Island and Providence Plantations, five in Connecticut, six in New-York, four in New-Jersey, eight in Pennsylvania, one in Delaware, six in Maryland, ten in Virginia, five in North-Carolina, five in South-Carolina, and three in Georgia.

Sect. 4. As the proportions of numbers in the different States will alter from time to time; as some of the States may hereafter be divided; as others may be enlarged by addition of territory; as two or more States may be united; as new States will be erected within the limits of the United States, the Legislature shall, in each of these cases, regulate the number of representatives by the number of inhabitants, according to the provisions herein after made, at the rate of one for every forty thousand.

Sect. 5. All bills for raising or appropriating money, and for fixing the salaries of the officers of government, shall originate in the House of Representatives, and shall not be altered or amended by the Senate. No money shall be drawn from the public Treasury, but in pursuance of appropriations that shall originate in the House of Representatives.

Sect. 6. The House of Representatives shall have the sole power of impeachment. It shall chuse its Speaker and other officers.

Sect. 7. Vacancies in the House of Representatives shall be supplied by writs of election from the executive authority of the State, in the representation from which they shall happen.

V.

The Constitution of the United States: A Delicate Balancing Act

Although the new Constitution called for a strong central government, the states also retained a great deal of power. This system of "dual sovereignty" (two powers) allowed both governments to exist at once.

The Constitution created at the Philadelphia convention gave the central government specific powers. The states, on the other hand, were to retain any government powers they already had had that were not specifically granted to the central government. This division of power between the central government and the state governments, known as the federal system of government, remains in place to this day.

The central government under the Constitution is divided into three branches: legislative, executive, and judicial. The legislative (lawmaking) branch of government is the Congress. The executive branch is led by the President, and is responsible for enforcing federal laws and carrying out national policies. The judicial branch, the national court system headed by the Supreme Court, is responsible for cases arising from federal and constitutional laws.

Each branch of government is granted specific areas of responsibility, but the Constitution also gives each branch some oversight of the others. This system of "checks and balances" between the branches of government is intended to prevent any branch from becoming too powerful.

Congress: The two-house compromise

The self-interests of the various states at the convention led to the formation of a unique legislative body. Large states argued that the number of representatives each state sent to the legislature (Congress) should be based on the states' population (how many people lived in each state). Southern states, which had large populations of slaves at the time, argued that they should be able to count the slaves when determining how many representatives they sent to Congress. Delegates from smaller states argued for equal representation for every state, regardless of its population. Delegates from the northern states, where slavery was far less common, however, opposed the use of slaves in determining representation.

The convention eventually reached a compromise, creating a Congress made up of two houses, or assemblies. In the upper house of Congress—the Senate—each state would be represented by two senators, giving the states equal standing. However, in the lower house of Congress—the House of Representatives—a state's representation would be determined by the relative size of its population (the larger a state's population, the more representatives that state sent to the House of Representatives). Bills (proposed laws) must be passed by both houses before they could become law.

Additionally, the Convention agreed that a state's population would be determined by counting the number of free persons (non-slaves) in the state and adding "three-fifths of all other Persons" [slaves] while "excluding Indians," who neither voted nor were taxed. (Slavery was abolished altogether in 1865 by the Thirteenth Amendment [see chapter thirteen]).

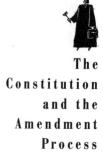

Article I, section 8 of the Constitution outlines most of the powers granted to Congress. These include the power to impose taxes, to provide for the common defense and general welfare of the United States, and to regulate commerce. Congress was also empowered to create a national currency (money), a postal system, and a system of courts below the Supreme Court. Only Congress can declare war and is given the power to raise and support an army and navy. More generally, the Constitution's "necessary and proper" clause states that Congress has the power "to make all laws which shall be necessary and proper for carrying into execution the foregoing powers, and all other powers vested by the Constitution in the government of the United States."

The president oversees many different aspects of running the country. Reproduced by permission of AP/Wide World Photos.

The Executive Branch: All the president's men

Under Article II of the Constitution, the president holds executive (or administrative) power. Presidents are elected to a four-year term by an Electoral College, made up of electors chosen by each of the states (see chapter twelve).

The president is the commander-in-chief of the nation's armed forces, and is responsible for ensuring that federal laws are "faithfully executed," which gives the president control over federal law enforcement agencies. The president also is responsible for appointing judges and federal officials and has the power to negotiate treaties (agreements) with other nations.

The vice president serves as president of the Senate and casts the deciding vote in any tie votes in that house. The vice president has few other powers, but must step in for the president if the president is unable to perform the executive duties.

The Judicial Branch: Supreme powers

Article III of the Constitution establishes the Supreme Court as the highest court in the United States. Congress may also create any lower courts it deems necessary. Federal judges are appointed for life, so that they will be less likely to give in to political pressure when deciding cases.

Federal courts hear cases arising from federal laws, or cases in which the federal government is involved, or where citizens from two different states are involved. The Supreme Court, however, generally hears cases only on appeal, that is, when a party in the case requests that the Court reconsider the ruling of a lower court. The Supreme Court's decisions cannot be appealed, and the Court serves as the final interpreter

The Supreme Court in 1868. Reproduced by permission of the Corbis Corporation (Bellevue).

of the laws of the United States, including all matters dealing with the Constitution and its amendments.

The Court consisted of six justices (judges) until 1869, when it was officially expanded to nine justices. In deciding cases, justices may write individual opinions (written explanations of the justice's reasoning in a case) or sign another justice's opinion. Regardless of how many opinions the Court issues in a case, its final ruling is decided by a simple vote of the justices.

Because it is the final interpreter of law in the United States, the Supreme Court has played a significant role in the history of the Constitution's various amendments.

Checks and balances: The branches' overlapping powers

As stated above, each of the three branches of government exercises some oversight of the others. The Senate must approve all treaties negotiated by the executive branch. While the president is commander-in-chief of the armed forces, only Congress can declare war. The president, on the other hand, may veto (reject) any bill passed by Congress. Once vetoed, a two-thirds majority in both houses of Congress must pass a bill for it to become law.

While the president appoints all federal judges and government officers, the Senate must also approve those appointments. Furthermore, the House of Representatives has the power to impeach (officially accuse of legal misconduct) judges and government officials. Once impeached, these officials (including the president) may be tried in the Senate, and if convicted may be removed from office.

Finally, the Supreme Court may use its power to interpret laws and the Constitution to strike down any laws or government actions it deems illegal or unconstitutional.

Ratifying the Constitution: A Question of Rights

Despite the Constitution's federal system of state and central government, and the system of checks and balances, many delegates to the Constitutional Convention worried that the new government would become too powerful. Toward the end of the convention, a debate began over whether the Constitution should include a bill of rights (a specific list of the people's rights).

James Madison drafted the original amendments that would become the Bill of Rights. Courtesy of the Library of Congress.

Anti-Federalists argued that without a bill of rights, the central government might eventually take away individual rights. The Federalists, however, argued that there was no need to spell out individual rights since the new government could only exercise those powers expressed in the Constitution.

According to Article VII of the Constitution, a minimum of nine of the thirteen states had to ratify the document before it could go into effect. In the months that followed the convention, Anti-Federalists continued to raise the issue of a bill of rights with the public. Having just fought to get rid of the powerful British government, many citizens were afraid of giving the new government too much power without some sort of declaration of the people's rights.

Federalists initially argued against the inclusion of a bill of rights. But in order to win approval for the new constitution, they eventually promised that Congress would add a bill of rights to the Constitution during its first session.

The first amendments: Crafting the Bill of Rights

The Federalists kept their word. From the hundreds of proposals made by the states, James Madison, now a representative to the House, drafted seventeen amendment proposals, which he presented to Congress

on June 8, 1789. Over the next three months, Congress revised Madison's suggestions into twelve amendment proposals, which were then passed to the states for ratification. While the states were considering the proposed amendments, Vermont became the fourteenth state on March 4, 1791. Under the rules set out in the Constitution, this meant that eleven states (three-fourths of the existing states) were needed to ratify the constitutional amendments.

Though two of the proposed amendments were rejected (one would later become the Twenty-seventh Amendment), on December 15, 1791, Virginia became the eleventh state to approve the ten amendments that became the Bill of Rights. These amendments set out specific limits to the exercise of government power while guaranteeing certain rights to citizens, especially in regard to court and police actions.

- The First Amendment prohibits Congress from passing any law that abridges (decreases) the existing freedom of speech, religion, or the press (the media).

- The Second Amendment guarantees the "people's right to keep and bear arms [weapons]."

- The Third Amendment limits the government's ability to quarter (or house) soldiers in private homes.

- The Fourth Amendment prohibits unreasonable search and seizure.

- The Fifth Amendment includes several protections for people accused of crimes, including protection against "double jeopardy" (being tried twice for the same crime) and the right not to testify against oneself in trial.

- The Sixth Amendment provides the right to a speedy trial by jury in criminal cases.

- The Seventh Amendment provides for jury trials in civil cases.

- The Eighth Amendment prohibits the setting of excessive bail and fines, and forbids cruel and unusual punishments.

- The Ninth Amendment states that the rights listed in the Constitution are not the only rights retained by the people.

- The Tenth Amendment states that any powers not specifically granted to the federal government are retained by the states and the people, unless the Constitution specifically prohibits the use of such powers.

The Changing Constitution: Proposing and Ratifying Constitutional Amendments

Those first additions and changes to the Constitution were made according to rules spelled out in the Constitution. In fact, Article V of the Constitution sets out two methods for amending the Constitution.

In the first method, Congress may propose an amendment with a two-thirds vote of both the Senate and the House of Representatives. If the proposal passes in both houses, the amendment must then be ratified by three-fourths of the states, either in state-wide conventions or by votes in the states' legislatures (law-making assemblies).

Under the second method, Congress can call for a constitutional convention for the proposal of new amendments. Congress can call for such a convention only if the legislatures from at least two-thirds of the states request that Congress do so.

Any proposals drafted at such a convention must then be ratified by three-fourths of the states. To date, however, the Constitution has only been amended through the first method.

Amending the Constitution is quite difficult. It requires an enormous degree of consensus (agreement) at the state and federal level. The

Abraham Lincoln worked to ensure the emancipation of slaves from their owners. Courtesy of the Library of Congress.

framers of the Constitution wanted to make sure that changes to the government were not made lightly. Indeed, in the two hundred-plus years since the Bill of Rights was ratified, only seventeen other amendments have been adopted by the states.

- The Eleventh Amendment (1798) prohibits the Supreme Court from hearing any lawsuits brought against one state by a citizen of another state.

- The Twelfth Amendment (1804) changed the way the president and vice president are elected. The amendment was drafted in response to the election of 1800. At the time, the offices of president and vice president were voted on separately. The party candidate who received the most votes would be president, and the candidate with the next highest number of votes would be vice president. In the election of 1800, one political party's presidential and vice presidential candidates accidentally received the same number of electoral votes for president, causing a great deal of confusion over who would serve as president.

- The Thirteenth (1865), Fourteenth (1868) and Fifteenth (1870) Amendments— which abolished slavery, required states to enforce their laws fairly, and extended the vote to black males—were all passed in the wake of America's bloody Civil War (1860–64) between the Northern and Southern states.

- The Sixteenth Amendment (1913) overrode a technicality in the Constitution, and made it legal for the federal government to implement an income tax.

- The Seventeenth Amendment (1913) provides for the direct election of senators by voters in each state. The Constitution originally gave state legislatures the power to appoint a state's senators.

- The Eighteenth (1919) and Twenty-first Amendments (1933) reflected America's changing attitudes toward alcoholic beverages. The Eighteenth Amendment outlawed the sale and transportation of liquor in the United States, reflecting the nation's growing temperance (anti-alcohol) movement. By 1933, though, American attitudes toward the sale of alcohol had shifted again, and the Twenty-first Amendment repealed (reversed) the ban on liquor.

- The Nineteenth Amendment (1920) extended the vote to women, after nearly a century of vigorous campaigning for female suffrage (the right to vote).

OPPOSITE PAGE

The government works to make sure that everyone gets a fair chance to vote in elections. This is a Braille ballot for a blind voter.

Reproduced by permission of AP/Wide World Photos.

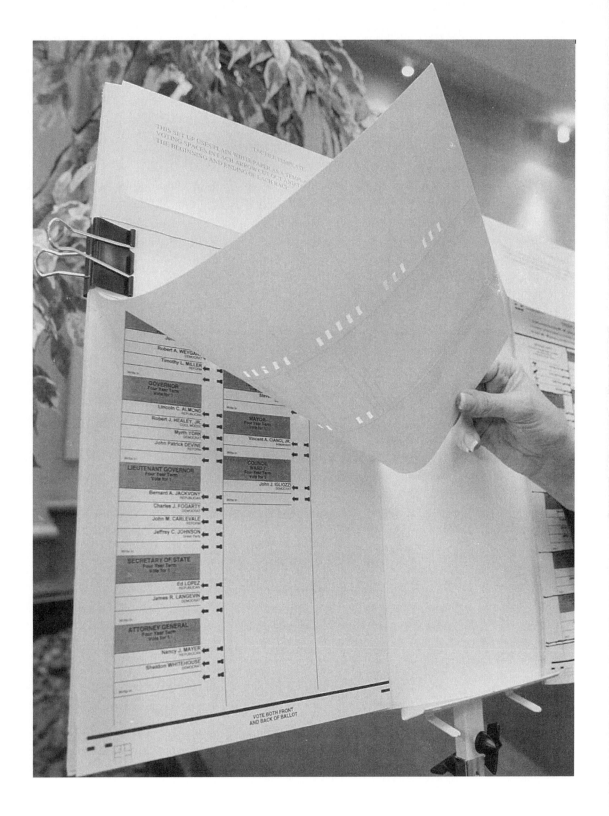

Introduction

- The Twentieth Amendment (1933) shortened the period between the time a person was elected to federal office and the time he or she took office.

- The Twenty-second Amendment (1951) prohibited any person from being elected to more than two terms as president, and was proposed after the death of Franklin D. Roosevelt, who was elected to four successive terms, beginning with the election of 1932.

- The Twenty-third Amendment (1961) gave residents of Washington D.C. (the nation's capital) the right to vote in presidential elections.

- The Twenty-fourth Amendment (1964) put an end to the practice of charging people a fee, or poll tax, to cast their vote in an election.

- The Twenty-fifth Amendment (1967) granted the president the power to nominate a new vice president whenever that office becomes vacant. The amendment also provides for the vice president to take over a president's duties when the president cannot perform those duties due to poor health or injury. This amendment was passed in the wake of the assassination of President John F. Kennedy in 1961. Vice President Lyndon B. Johnson assumed the presidency, leaving the vice president's office vacant for the remainder of the term.

- The Twenty-sixth Amendment (1971) lowered the legal voting age from twenty-one to eighteen in all elections.

- The Twenty-seventh Amendment (1992) was one of the original twelve amendments proposed for the Bill of Rights in 1789. However, the amendment, which prohibits any pay raise Congress votes for itself from taking effect until the following election, was not ratified until the 1990s, when the issue became a popular political issue.

Additionally, Congress has passed a number of proposals for amendments that failed to be ratified by the necessary three-fourths of the states (see chapter twenty-eight).

Certainly, the Constitution's enduring power is due in part to the fact that the framers provided a method of amending the document when necessary. What is remarkable in discussing the Constitutional amendments, however, is how very rarely the American people have found it necessary to do so.

Constitutional Amendments

First Amendment

Congress shall make no law respecting an establishment of religion, or prohibiting the free exercise thereof; or abridging the freedom of speech, or of the press, or the right of the people peaceably to assemble, and to petition the Government for a redress of grievances.

Free speech; a free press; the separation of church and state; freedom to assemble and to petition the government: The First Amendment contains all of these most cherished rights. As we'll see, none of these rights to political, religious or artistic freedom are unlimited. The government must weigh an individual's freedom of expression against community interests, concern for public safety, and national security interests.

After years of being ignored by government and the courts, the First Amendment has emerged as the amendment that the public most closely associates with the Bill of Rights, standing as a statement of the core values of American freedom and democracy.

From One Bill of Rights to Another

In 1689, the English Parliament (Great Britain's government) enacted the English Bill of Rights, which sharply limited the power of the king and queen and gave greater power to Parliament itself. The Bill of Rights listed fundamental liberties, including: freedom of elections; freedom of debate in Parliament; freedom from excessive bail, and cruel and unusual punishments (see chapter eight); and the right to petition (ask) the government for correction of public grievances (complaints). As British subjects, colonists in Britain's North American colonies also felt entitled to the liberties listed in the English Bill of Rights.

RATIFICATION FACTS

PROPOSED: Submitted by Congress to the states on September 25, 1789, along with the other nine amendments that comprise the Bill of Rights.

RATIFICATION: Ratified by the required three-fourths of states (eleven of fourteen) on December 15, 1791. Declared to be part of the Constitution on December 15, 1791.

RATIFYING STATES: New Jersey, November 20, 1789; Maryland, December 19, 1789; North Carolina, December 22, 1789; South Carolina, January 19, 1790; New Hampshire, January 25, 1790; Delaware, January 28, 1790; New York, February 24, 1790; Pennsylvania, March 10, 1790; Rhode Island, June 7, 1790; Vermont, November 3, 1791; Virginia, December 15, 1791 (amendment adopted).

During the 1700s, ideas about individual rights grew in popularity. Such ideas were outlined by the English philosopher John Locke in *Two Treatises on Government* (1690). Locke argued that people are born completely free, but give up some of their freedom to governments for the good of society. However, since a government's power comes directly from the people, a government must always act for their good. Otherwise, people must have the right to change the government.

Revolution to Constitution

Locke's ideas helped spur the American Revolutionary War (1775–1783) in which the thirteen American colonies fought for their independence from the British government. Colonists argued that the British government repeatedly violated rights established by the English Bill of Rights. For instance, petitioning the government to address grievances was made nearly impossible because of laws that made speaking against the government a crime.

The colonies' growing dissatisfaction with the British government was revealed in an early case concerning freedom of the press. John Peter Zenger (1697–1746) was the publisher of the *New York Weekly Journal.* Zenger was charged with seditious libel (speaking out against the government) after printing a series of articles critical of New York's colonial governor. Although the law was clearly against Zenger, the jury of colonists in his 1735 trial refused to convict him.

War broke out between Great Britain and the colonies in 1775. In June of 1776, Virginia adopted the Virginia Declaration of Rights. This colonial version of the Bill of Rights listed specific liberties that could not be taken away by government, such as, freedom of the press, and the free exercise of religion. In July of 1776, the colonists issued a formal Declaration of Independence. It listed complaints against the British government, and asserted the people's right to change their government.

A NEW GOVERNMENT: OLD RIGHTS. In 1781, the colonies defeated the British Army and formed a limited national government under a document known as the Articles of Confederation. The Articles established a national legislature (lawmaking body), but did not create a court system or executive branch to enforce government policies. Calls for a stronger national (federal) government led to the adoption of the Constitution of the United States (see Introduction) in 1788. The new Constitution created a powerful federal government with the power to collect taxes, declare

First Amendment

The pilgrims came to America looking for greater freedoms.
Reproduced by permission of Archive Photos, Inc.

**First
Amendment**

war, and maintain armed forces. The new government's powers were divided between:

- the executive branch, headed by the president, which carries out government policies;

- the legislative branch (Congress) made up of elected representatives in the House of Representatives and state-appointed representatives in the Senate; and

- the judicial branch (courts) headed by the Supreme Court (see below).

Before the states ratified (approved) the Constitution, many people worried that the new government would become too powerful. Many argued that the Constitution should have a list of guaranteed liberties similar to Virginia's Declaration of Rights. The Constitution was ratified after supporters agreed that a bill of rights would be drafted during the first session of Congress.

Congress met for the first time in 1789. James Madison (1751–1836) was a member of the House of Representatives from Virginia. (He later became the fourth President of the United States.) Madison wrote and introduced seventeen proposals for amendments that guaranteed numerous rights. Congress reworked Madison's proposals, and passed twelve amendments to the Constitution on September 25, 1789. The states ratified ten of the amendments (including what became the First Amendment) in 1791, thereby establishing America's own Bill of Rights.

Interpreting the Law of the Land

As set up by the Constitution, the Supreme Court is the highest court in the United States. The Court originally consisted of six justices (judges), but was expanded to nine justices in 1869. The Supreme Court is responsible for the final interpretation of laws (including amendments to the Constitution) in the United States.

Most cases are heard by trial courts, or by appellate courts that consider appeals. (An appeal is a legal request for a higher court to reconsider a ruling in a case.) The Supreme Court may hear any case or reconsider any lower court ruling.

In deciding cases, Supreme Court justices may write individual opinions, or sign another justice's opinion. An opinion is a written explanation of the justice's reasoning about a case's ruling. Regardless of how many opinions the Court issues in a case, the final ruling is decided by a simple vote of all the justices. It is also not uncommon for the Supreme Court to change its interpretation of law, often reflecting changes in American society.

Applying the Bill of Rights to the States

The Bill of Rights was originally intended only for the federal government. States were allowed to manage their own affairs, without regard for the first ten amendments. For example, the governments of Connecticut and Massachusetts continued to run state-supported Congregational churches into the 1800s, even though the First Amendment restricted Congress from establishing or sponsoring a religion.

The Fourteenth Amendment (ratified by the states in 1868) contains the Due Process and Equal Protection Clauses (see chapter fourteen). These clauses require states to protect the "life, liberty, and property" with due process (fair and equal application) of the law. Over the years, the Supreme Court has interpreted these clauses to mean that various parts of the Bill of Rights do apply to state and local governments in addition to the federal government. Several of the First Amendment's clauses have been "incorporated" by the Supreme Court into this interpretation of the Fourteenth Amendment.

No Government in Religion, No Religion in Government

There are two clauses in the First Amendment that protect religious freedom:

- The Establishment Clause ("Congress shall make no law respecting an establishment of religion ... ") prohibits the establishment of an "official" state church and bans the government from taking any actions that may favor one religion over another.

- The Free Exercise Clause (Congress shall make no law "prohibiting the free exercise" of religion) bans the government from undue interference with a person's right to practice their faith. The Supreme Court, however, has ruled that the government may limit religious practices that are deemed harmful to society.

Building a wall of separation

In 1802, President Thomas Jefferson (1743–1826) argued that the First Amendment called for a "wall of separation between Church and

*The celebration
acceptance of many
different religions
and beliefs is part of
what makes America
so diverse.* Reproduced
by permission of the Corbis
Corporation (Bellevue).

State." Over the years, the Supreme Court has helped build this wall. The
Court has consistently ruled that in addition to prohibiting the establishment of a government sponsored religion, the Establishment Clause also
prohibits the government from taking any action that aids any religion, or
prefers one religion over another. Many religious freedom cases have
focused on the activities of public and parochial (religious) schools.

BUSFARE, BUT NO SALARIES. In *Everson v. Board of Education* (1947), the
Supreme Court used the Due Process Clause of the Fourteenth
Amendment (see chapter fourteen) to apply the Establishment Clause to

the actions of state and local governments. The case involved a public school board's decision to pay for the cost of transporting children to and from Catholic schools. This was part of a larger program that paid the transportation costs of children in public (government run) and private schools.

The Supreme Court ruled that the government money could pay the costs of transporting children to religious institutions (the Catholic schools) because the state had an interest in transporting children "regardless of their religion ... to and from accredited schools." Since *Everson,* the Supreme Court has upheld state laws requiring public school districts to lend textbooks on secular (non-religious) subjects to students in private and parochial schools.

The Court was less receptive to state laws that gave direct financial assistance to religious schools. In *Lemon v. Kurtzman* (1971), the Court struck down laws that used public funds to help pay teachers in parochial schools.

KNEELING AND KNOWLEDGE. Prior to 1962, many states required public schools to begin the school day with a prayer or a Bible reading. For example, the state of New York developed a prayer that had been approved by Protestant, Catholic, and Jewish leaders. Student participation in the prayer was strictly voluntary. Nevertheless, the Supreme Court ruled in *Engel v. Vitale* (1962) that the prayer violated the Establishment Clause. In *Abington School District v. Schempp* (1963), the Court struck down voluntary Bible readings or recitations of the Lord's Prayer in public schools. In both cases the Court ruled that these practices served only religious purposes, and therefore violated the Establishment Clause.

Some religious groups reacted quite vocally against these rulings. However, many religious groups applauded the decision, because they believed that a strong wall between church and state prevented the government from favoring one religion over another. In any case, the Supreme Court has ruled consistently against similar religious practices in public schools. In *Stone v. Graham* (1980), the Court struck down a Kentucky law that required the posting of the Ten Commandments in public school classrooms. In *Wallace v. Jaffree* (1985), the Court ruled that an Alabama law requiring public school students to observe a moment of silence "for the purpose of meditation or voluntary prayer" was unconstitutional. In *Lee v. Weisman* (1992), the Court ruled that a religious prayer read at a public school graduation violated the Establishment Clause.

The separation of church and state ensures that the government is not showing favor to any one religion.

Reproduced by permission of Field Mark Publications.

RELIGIOUS ACTIVITIES ON PUBLIC FACILITIES. While the government cannot establish religious activities in public schools, the Court ruled in *Widmar v. Vincent* (1981) that it is unconstitutional for a state university (or school) to prohibit a religious group from using its facilities if the facilities are also open for other organizations to use.

Providing special education at parochial schools

Under the Elementary and Secondary Education Act of 1965, all educationally and economically disadvantaged children are entitled to publicly funded remedial (special courses designed to help students overcome learning obstacles) education services, regardless of whether they attend public or private schools. Many school systems, including the New York City school system, complied with the law by paying public school teachers to conduct special training at private and parochial schools. In *Aguilar v. Felton* (1985), the Court ruled that New York City's practice was unconstitutional because it *could* lead to the kind of entanglement between church and state that the Establishment Clause prohibits.

In *Agostini v. Felton* (1997), however, the Supreme Court overruled its *Aguilar v. Felton* decision. In the 1997 case, the Court ruled that a program was not unconstitutional if it *might* lead to an entanglement of church and state, only if it actually did so. The Court found no evidence that New York's practice of allowing public school teachers to teach remedial education in parochial schools led to such entanglements, and ruled that the program could be reinstated.

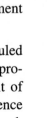

The Free Exercise Clause

While the Establishment Clause clearly limits government's role in supporting religious activities, the Free Exercise Clause limits the government's ability to restrict activities performed for religious purposes. However, from the earliest case concerning free exercise of religion, the Supreme Court has given the government broad power to limit religious practices.

HOW MANY WIVES CAN ONE MAN HAVE? In *Reynolds v. United States* (1878), a member of the Church of Jesus Christ of Latter-day Saints (Mormons) argued that a law outlawing polygamy (marriage to more than one person at the same time) interfered with his religious duty to have several wives. The Court, however, ruled that while Congress could not pass laws that tried to control religious belief, it could pass laws that controlled certain behaviors that were "in violation of social duties or (that undermined) good order."

The Court ruled that a law outlawing multiple marriages did not violate the First Amendment since the law applied equally to everyone. Soon after the ruling, the Mormon leadership abandoned the practice of approving multiple marriages. Even with the Free Exercise Clause, *Reynolds* established that the government may enforce laws that conflict with a person's religious beliefs if there is a compelling (strong) interest in doing so.

GOING DOOR TO DOOR WITH GOD. In *Cantwell v. Connecticut* (1940), the Supreme Court applied the Free Exercise Clause to the states through the Fourteenth Amendment's Due Process Clause (see chapter fourteen). The

Constitutional Amendments

ruling struck down a state law that prohibited religious groups from going door to door with their message unless they first obtained approval from a state agency. The Court found that requiring state approval of these religious activities violated the Free Exercise Clause.

A BALANCING ACT. The Court ruled against state interference again in *Sherbert v. Verner* (1963). In *Verner*, an unemployed woman refused to take jobs that required her to work on Saturdays. It was against her religion as a Seventh Day Adventist to work on Saturdays. When she couldn't find other work, the woman tried to collect unemployment compensation from the state. The state refused her claim, arguing that the woman had turned down suitable work.

The Supreme Court, however, weighed the government's interest against the woman's religious liberty, and found that the state had no compelling interest in insisting a person work on Saturdays. Therefore, the Court ruled that the state was unnecessarily limiting the woman's religious freedom by refusing to pay her unemployment benefits.

A HOLE IN THE WALL? The "wall of separation" between church and state prevents the government from taking part in religious activities, but it doesn't prevent religious leaders from participating in government. In *McDaniel v. Paty et al.* (1978), the Court ruled that a Tennessee law prohibiting "[m]inister[s] of the Gospel, or priest[s] of any denomination whatever" from running for state office was unconstitutional. The Court ruled that the law violated the First Amendment because it required a person to give up a right—the right to seek political office—in order to fully participate in his or her religion.

DRUGS AND RELIGION. The Free Exercise Clause does not permit religious groups to engage in conduct the government considers harmful to public health, safety, or morality. For instance, in *Employment Division, Department of Human Resources of Oregon v. Smith,* (1990), the Court upheld an Oregon law that prohibited members of the Native American Church from using peyote (an illegal drug) for traditional religious purposes. The Court ruled that as long the law outlawing peyote was not passed specifically to limit a religious practice, the government could limit the drug's use for religious and non-religious activities alike.

Matters of conscience and the First Amendment

In some cases an individual may choose not to follow a law that seriously conflicts with the person's religious values or conscience (personal beliefs about right and wrong).

OPPOSITE PAGE:

The freedom of religion makes it possible for many different religions to exist and be practiced around the nation, such as Mormonism in this Salt Lake City temple.

Reproduced by permission of the Utah Travel Council.

First Amendment

Many faiths follow beliefs that may be considered unconventional, such as the Jewish observance of the Sabbath beginning at sundown on Friday. No law could be made forcing a person of Jewish faith to work on his or her Sabbath.

SALUTING THE FLAG. In *Minersville School District v. Gobitis* (1940), the Supreme Court originally upheld a state law that required public school students to salute the American flag. The Jehovah's Witnesses religious sect argued that their religion prohibited them from saluting the flag, because it was a form of worshipping "graven images." However, three years later in *West Virginia State Board of Education v. Barnette,* the Court overruled its *Gobitis* decision. The Court found that the First Amendment prohibited the government from forcing people to demonstrate patriotism (loyalty to the country).

CONSCIETOUS OBJECTORS. Throughout U.S. history, the federal government has instituted drafts to provide manpower to the armed services. A draft is a lottery: men are selected by chance, and required to serve in the armed services. Congress has excused men who object to war on religious grounds from serving in the military. During times when a draft is in place, a conscientious objector may be excused from military service if he signs a statement that states: "I am, by reason of my religious training and belief, conscientiously opposed to participation in war of any form."

In *Welsh v. United States* (1970), the Supreme Court ruled that even a person with strong non-religious objections to war may be excused

from military service. The objections must be based on personal beliefs about right and wrong, and be held with the same intensity as more conventional (standard) religious beliefs. However, this ruling did not allow a person with political objections to a particular war (as opposed to conscientious objections to *all* wars) to qualify as a conscientious objector.

From a Whisper to a Scream

Despite the First Amendment requirement that Congress make no law "abridging (shortening or weakening) the freedom of speech," the Supreme Court has consistently ruled that the government may limit or even ban certain types of speech in various situations. The type of control the government may exercise often depends on what *kind* of speech is being considered. As we'll see, different types of speech have been treated very differently by the government and the courts.

Subversive and seditious speech

Ten years after Congress passed the First Amendment protecting free speech, it passed the Alien and Sedition Acts of 1798. The two acts, passed with the backing of President John Adams (1735–1826), restricted written and spoken criticism of the government (seditious speech). Thomas Jefferson (who was Adams' vice president) objected to the acts. Jefferson argued that nowhere in the Constitution was Congress given the power to punish seditious speech. However, the laws were never reviewed by the Supreme Court. The Alien and Sedition Acts expired on March 3, 1801—just before Jefferson took office as the third president of the United States. Once in office, Jefferson pardoned all those convicted under the acts.

Federal and state governments continued to limit certain types of speech. It was illegal in southern states to speak out against slavery before the Civil War (1861–1865). (The Civil War was fought between the Northern, or Union, states and the Southern, or Confederate, states over issues such as state and federal power, and the future of slavery in the United States.) During the war, the federal government censored what newspapers could print about the war, and took outspoken critics of the government to court. However, the Supreme Court did not rule on any of these matters.

TESTING FOR DANGER. In 1917, the United States entered World War I (1914–1918). (World War I was a war fought between a number of

**First
Amendment**

European nations and their allies). The federal government instituted a draft that provided soldiers for the overseas war effort. Many citizens protested the draft, and argued that the United States should not be involved in "foreign wars."

Congress passed the Espionage Act of 1917 and the Sedition Act of 1918 with the intention of ending such criticisms. Under these acts, Charles T. Schenck was arrested for circulating pamphlets that urged men to resist the draft. The pamphlets suggested actions that seemed legal, such as petitioning the government to do away with the draft. In *Schenck v. United States* (1919), however, the Supreme Court ruled that the pamphlets were not entitled to First Amendment protection.

"The question in every case," the Court ruled, "is whether the words used are used ... to create a clear and present danger that ... Congress has a right to prevent." In other words, if the Court found that Schenk's pamphlets could harm the nation—by undermining the draft—and ruled that they were not protected by the First Amendment. The Court went on to argue that "[W]hen a nation is at war many things that might be said in time of peace" cannot be protected by "any constitutional right."

In the 1950s and 1960s, Senator Joseph McCarthy worked to expose Communists in America and have them black-listed or arrested for conspiring to overthrow the government.

Reproduced by permission of AP/Wide World Photos.

UNCLEAR AND ABSENT DANGER? After *Schenk,* the Court left behind the "clear and present danger" test. In several cases, the Court allowed the suppression of speech that it admitted posed no "clear and present danger," but that the Court found *might* eventually be harmful to the country's interests.

In 1940, Congress enacted the Internal Security Act, commonly known as the Smith Act. The act made it illegal not only to conspire (plan) to overthrow the government, but even to advocate (argue for) the overthrowing of the government. (Planning to overthrow the government represents a clear and present danger to the country. Supporting such a plan poses a less immediate threat to the country, but is still considered a serious action.)

The Supreme Court upheld the constitutionality of the Smith Act in *Dennis v. United States* (1951). The Court found Eugene Dennis and ten others guilty of violating the act by carrying out the schemes of the American Communist Party (a political organization that, at the time, was thought to support the violent overthrow of the U.S. government).

BACK TO THE "PRESENT." In 1969, the Court returned to the "clear and present danger" test for determining whether the government could suppress anti-government speech. In *Brandenburg v. Ohio,* the Court ruled that an Ohio law that banned arguing for the use of illegal conduct was unconstitutional. (The Supreme Court had first applied the Free Speech Clause (see above) to state and local governments in *Fiske v. Kansas* [1927].) In its decision, the Court stated that "the constitutional guarantees of free speech and free press do not permit a State to forbid the mere advocacy of violence or breaking the law, unless the advocacy is intended to incite [immediate lawless action]."

Statements without words

Symbolic speech is nonverbal (neither spoken nor written) actions that communicate a message. For instance, marching to protest a government policy is considered symbolic expression. The Supreme Court first gave symbolic speech First Amendment protection in *Stromberg v. California* (1931). In *Stromberg*, the Court ruled that a California law prohibiting the display of a red flag as an "... emblem of opposition to organized government" was unconstitutional.

In *United States v. O'Brien* (1968), the Supreme Court upheld the conviction of David Paul O'Brien for illegally burning his draft card at a rally protesting the Vietnam War. (The Vietnam War [1954–1975] was a war between the government of South Vietnam, aided by the United

**First
Amendment**

FIGHTING WORDS AND BURNING CROSSES

The dividing line between protected and unprotected speech can be narrow. The First Amendment protects freedom of speech made in public places such as streets, plazas, and parks. However, in certain circumstances the government may limit public speech if it provokes anger in a listener, or disrupts peace and order.

In *Chaplinsky v. New Hampshire* (1942), the Supreme Court ruled that words that are not essential to the expression of an idea, and are solely intended to incite violence, are not protected by the First Amendment. When Walter Chaplinsky was arrested he called an officer a Fascist (a person who supports a type of government with a rigid dictatorship), and said the local government was Fascist. He was convicted of violating a state law that prohibited a addressing a person with "offensive, derisive (ridiculing) or annoying" words in a street or public place.

The Supreme Court affirmed the conviction. The Court reasoned that Chaplinsky's words were an invitation to fight, and would have caused a breach of the peace. Justice Frank Murphy wrote for a unanimous court, and stated that "fighting words—those which by their very utterance inflict injury or tend to incite an immediate breach of the peace" are not protected by the First Amendment.

The Court has since made clear that so-called "fighting words" is not just offensive speech. In fact, crude or insensitive language that just offends, or hurts the feelings of another person, but that doesn't elicit

States, and South Vietnamese rebels aided by the communist government of North Vietnam. American involvement in the war was heavily protested in the United States during the late 1960s and early 1970s.)

O'Brien claimed that burning his card was symbolic speech protected by the First Amendment. But the Court ruled that any speech, symbolic or otherwise, could be regulated if the government had a substantial interest in doing so. In this case, the Court found that the government had a legitimate interest in requiring men to carry their draft cards to ensure the proper functioning of the military draft.

The same year, the Court ruled that the government did not have a legitimate interest in suppressing another form of symbolic protest. In

(provoke) an angry or violent response, is usually protected by the First Amendment.

But the government must be careful even when it acts to limit true "fighting words." In *R.A.V. v. City of St. Paul, Minnesota,* (1992), the Supreme Court had to determine whether a statute (law) that outlawed cross burning violated an individual's freedom of expression under the First Amendment.

In 1990, the city of St. Paul, Minnesota, enacted the "Bias-Motivated Crime Ordinance," which stated that "Whoever places on public or private property a symbol, object ... or graffiti, including, but not limited to, a burning cross or Nazi swastika" and who has reason to know that this display will arouse anger or alarm in others based on "race, color, creed, religion or gender" shall be guilty of a misdemeanor (minor crime).

In June of 1990, several teenagers set a wooden cross on fire in a black family's yard. The teens were arrested and charged under the Bias-Motivated Crime Ordinance. The Supreme Court unanimously ruled that the ordinance violated the First Amendment. According to the Court's ruling, the city law only prohibited fighting words that insulted or provoked violence based on race, color, creed, religion, or gender. Justice Scalia noted that a speaker who expressed fighting words in connection with a political party, union membership, or homosexuality could not be prosecuted under the ordinance. Because the ordinance prohibited the actions of speakers who expressed certain ideas, it violated the First Amendment's protection of free speech.

Tinker v. Des Moines Independent Community School District (1969), high school officials suspended high school students for wearing black arm bands to protest the United States involvement in the Vietnam War. In its decision, the Court found that the wearing of arm bands was "akin to 'pure speech' which ... is entitled to comprehensive protection under the First Amendment ....," and that public school's had no legitimate interest in banning the arm bands.

FLAG BURNING. The United States flag has often been used by political protesters as a way to express opposition to government policies. Though the Supreme Court heard several cases involving flag burning in the 1960s and 1970s, the Court did not specifically rule on the issue of flag burning as a form of symbolic speech until *Texas v. Johnson* (1989). In that case, Gregory Johnson was arrested after he burned a United States flag outside the 1984 Republican National Convention in Dallas, Texas. He was convicted of violating a Texas law prohibiting flag desecration (not treating the flag as sacred). The U.S. Supreme Court ruled it was clear that "Johnson was convicted for engaging in expressive conduct." The Court found the state of Texas had no compelling interest in preventing flag burning except to stifle free political expression.

In reaction to *Texas v. Johnson,* Congress passed the Federal Flag Protection Act of 1989. The act made flag burning a federal crime. But in

*Many protesters
exercised their
right to free speech
during the Vietnam
War to express
their disapproval.*
Courtesy of the Library
of Congress.

United States v. Eichman (1990), the Court ruled that the act was unconstitutional, because it suppressed free expression without proving that the government had any compelling interest in doing so.

"I know it when I see it"

Obscenity is a legal term for a wide variety of expression that may be offensive to a community's moral standards (principle's of right and wrong). Obscenity may include pornography (sexual content in books, magazines, films, and recordings), nude dancing, or even "dirty" comedy routines. The Supreme Court has ruled that strictly obscene speech is not protected by the First Amendment. However, defining what is and is not obscene has proved a difficult task.

Supreme Court Justice Potter Stewart famously expressed this problem in *Jacobellis v. Ohio* (1964), "I know it when I see it."

ALL OR NOTHING? In 1873, Congress passed the Comstock Law. The law made it illegal to send or receive "obscene," "lewd," or "lascivious" (lustful) publications through the U.S. mail. Under the law, if a judge or jury determined that even a single passage of the publication was obscene, the publication was not protected by the First Amendment.

In *Roth v. United States* (1957), the Supreme Court changed the test for obscenity. Under the Court's ruling, materials were deemed obscene if they were found to be "utterly without redeeming social importance" and if the average person in a community would consider the material "as a whole" as obscene.

The Supreme Court added more requirements to the definition of obscenity in a 1966 case involving the bawdy (racy) English novel *Fanny Hill*. In *Memoirs v. Massachusetts,* the Court concluded that to establish obscenity, the material must be "utterly without redeeming social value," and "patently offensive because it affronts (insults) contemporary community standards relating to the description of sexual matters." The "utterly" without value requirement made prosecution in *Roth* and *Memoirs* difficult. Many defendants successfully argued that sexually explicit books or films also had literary or artistic value.

CHILD PORNOGRAPHY. One area of obscenity the Supreme Court has had no trouble defining is child pornography. In *New York v. Ferber* (1982), the Supreme Court held that child pornography (materials that show children in sexual situations) is not protected by the First Amendment, and that the government could ban the production of such materials. In *Osborne v. Ohio* (1990) the Court went even further, and allowed laws that prohibited the possession or viewing of child pornography.

PORNOGRAPHY ONLINE. Other forms of pornography have been protected by the Supreme Court. With the growth of the Internet in the 1990s, it became easier to distribute and receive pornographic pictures and other materials. In 1996, Congress passed the Communications Decency Act (CDA). The act prohibited the "knowing" distribution of obscene and indecent material to persons under eighteen through computer networks or other telecommunications media.

However, in *Reno v. American Civil Liberties Union* (1997), the Supreme Court found that the CDA violated the First Amendment. The CDA effectively made it illegal to distribute sexually explicit materials to adults as well as children. The ruling recognized the importance of "protecting children from harmful materials." However, the law went too far in limiting free speech. The Court pointed out that a number of systems have been developed to help parents limit their children's access to objectionable material on the Internet.

*Larry Flynt (center)
is the publisher of
the pornographic
magazine, Hustler.*
Reproduced by permission of
AP/Wide World Photos.

Pitching, pushing, and selling

Until the 1970s, the Supreme Court viewed advertisements and other commercial speech as forms of economic activity open to regulation by Congress. Local governments were free to restrict advertising. Many state and local laws prohibited the advertisement of prescription drug prices, liquor, and the professional services of attorneys or doctors.

In *Virginia State Board of Pharmacy v. Virginia Citizens Consumer Council* (1976), the Court struck down a Virginia law that prohibited the advertising of prescription drug prices. The Court found that even though the state could prohibit false and misleading advertisements, consumers had a strong First Amendment interest in the free flow of information. In a similar case, *Bates v. State Bar of Arizona* (1977), the Court ruled that ads for lawyers were also protected by the First Amendment, and could not be banned.

PROMOTING VICE? The Court has allowed the government to control certain types of ads. In *Posadas de Puerto Rico Associates v. Tourism Co. of P[uerto] R[ico]* (1986), the Court prohibited ads that invited Puerto Rican residents to gamble in local casinos. The Court found that the Puerto Rican government had an interest in reducing the demand for casino gambling among its citizens. Regulating gambling ads achieved that objective. The Court also pointed out that since the Puerto Rican legislature had the legal power to ban gambling altogether, it certainly had the lesser power to ban advertising of casino gambling.

Limiting broadcast speech

Unlike print media, radio and television broadcasts may be regulated for content. The federal government owns the broadcasting frequencies on behalf of the citizens of the United States, and licenses the frequencies to radio and television stations. The Federal Communications Commission (FCC) was established by the Communications Act of 1934. The FCC issues licenses to radio and television stations, and permits the stations to use specific frequencies to transmit programming. The FCC has the authority to regulate broadcasts of allegedly obscene or indecent material.

The Supreme Court has upheld FCC regulations banning obscene material, since obscenity is not protected by the First Amendment. In *FCC v. Pacifica Foundation* (1978), the Court permitted the FCC to prohibit the broadcasting of material that is "patently offensive," and either "sexual" or "excretory," during times when children are presumed to be in the audience.

**First
Amendment**

TWENTY-FOUR HOUR NUDE TV. These restrictions, however, do not necessarily apply to cable programming. Cable shows are not broadcast over public airwaves, but are instead transmitted through privately owned cable lines. In *Playboy v. United States* (2000), the Court struck down a section of the federal Telecommunications Act of 1996. The section required cable channels that transmitted sexually explicit materials to "fully scramble" their signals, or to restrict their transmission hours to times when children were unlikely to be viewing, such as the hours between ten P.M. and six A.M.

However, the Court found there were other ways to keep sexually explicit programming from reaching children without interfering with the cable companies right to free expression. For instance, cable companies have the ability to block any channel from reaching an individual cable subscribers home if the individual requests it.

Breaking News and Broken Promises

The First Amendment protection of a free press is, of course, closely connected to the broader protection of free speech. However, there are certain issues surrounding free expression that pertain specifically to the press.

- the amount an individual or a political action committee (PAC) may spend in support of, or in opposition to, a candidate, if these groups are independent of a candidate. (PACs are organizations formed by any group that is not identified with an individual candidate for the purpose of furthering political goals.)

The Court stated that "virtually every means of communicating ideas in today's mass society requires the expenditure of money." Therefore, the expenditure of money for political expression is protected by the First Amendment.

Since the *Buckley* decision PACs are not legally limited in their fund raising. They have become vehicles for major campaign spending, and many fear their political influence over candidates has risen as well. During the 1990s, the call for campaign finance reform grew louder, but the "money is speech" reasoning of *Buckley* provides a major roadblock to any meaningful changes in the way political campaigns are run.

Prior restraint

When government prohibits the expression of certain ideas before they are even published, it is exercising prior restraint. This has often been regarded as the ultimate form of censorship, because it allows government not only to punish speech, but to keep certain ideas from being heard at all. A limit on prior restraint is the heart of the First Amendment's protection of a free press.

This understanding became official in *Near v. Minnesota* (1931). In *Near*, the U.S. Supreme Court struck down a Minnesota state law that gave government officials the power to stop publication of any "malicious, scandalous and defamatory newspaper, magazine or other periodical." This was the first case in which the Court interpreted the Due Process Clause of the Fourteenth Amendment to hold that state and local governments must obey the First Amendment's Free Press Clause. The Court ruled the Minnesota law unconstitutional, and called it "the essence of censorship."

NATIONAL SECURITY AND PRIOR RESTRAINT. However, the *Near* decision did not provide an absolute protection against all prior restraint. For example, the Court pointed out that in time of war, the government could prohibit any publication of "the sailing dates of [navy ships] or

the number and location of troops," or other matters that threatened national security.

But national security interests are hard to prove. In the case of *New York Times Co. v. United States*(1971), the government sought to prevent the *New York Times* and the *Washington Post* newspapers from publishing excerpts of a classified study on the history of the United States involvement in the Vietnam War. The government argued that publishing the so-called "Pentagon Papers" would hurt national security interests. The Supreme Court ruled against the government. The Court found efforts to block publication of the papers amounted to unconstitutional prior restraint. The Court ruled there was no national security interests blocking the publication since the papers dealt with events that were all several years old.

CENSORSHIP IN SCHOOLS? While the right to a free press is one of the first rights taught in public schools, the right does not always apply to student newspapers. In *Hazelwood School District v. Kuhlmeier* (1988), the Supreme Court upheld a public school principal's decision to remove controversial material about teen pregnancy and divorce from the school's newspaper. The Court ruled that educators could exercise some editorial control over school run newspapers, but only when such control was "reasonably related to legitimate (educational) concerns."

"It ain't necessarily so"

Libel consists of injuring a person's reputation by reporting false-hoods about that person. A person injured by such actions may sue the person or group responsible for the libel. However, since the 1960s, the Supreme Court has made it harder to sue publishers, editors, and writers for libel.

In 1960, Dr. Martin Luther King, Jr. (1929–1968) and other civil rights leaders sought to end segregation in Montgomery, Alabama. They participated in events such as public marches to raise awareness of the Civil Rights cause, but were met with fierce resistance from Montgomery public officials. They placed a full-page advertisement in the *New York Times* stating that thousands of Southern African-American students were engaging in nonviolent demonstrations in favor of civil rights. The advertisement went on to state that the demonstrations had suffered a "wave of terror" because of state and local governments. Events backing up this charge were described, but no particular public official was named.

L. B. Sullivan was the commissioner responsible for supervising the Montgomery police department. He filed a libel suit against four of the civil rights leaders and the *New York Times* in Alabama state court. Sullivan alleged (declared) that the advertisement libeled him, because it implied (suggested) that he was responsible for the outrageous conduct of the officers under his command.

This became the case of the *New York Times v. Sullivan* (1964). In *Sullivan,* the Supreme Court ruled that the ad was protected by the First Amendment. The Court stated that "debate on public issues should be uninhibited, robust, and wide-open, and ... may well include vehement (very passionate), caustic (hostile), and sometimes unpleasantly sharp attacks on government and public officials." The Court maintained that some erroneous statements are inevitable in free debate, and must be protected if freedom of expression is to have the "breathing space" it needs to survive.

According to the ruling, a public official could only sue for libel if a libelous statement about the official was made with "'actual malice'— that is, with knowledge that it was false or with reckless disregard of whether it was false or not." As long as there is an "absence of malice" (ill will) on the part of the press, public officials cannot sue the press for publication of false statements about them.

Who said that?

In order to protect a free press, publishers and journalists have argued that reporters have an absolute right to keep the identity of their sources secret. They argue that without such a right, the press will not be able to obtain information vital to the public. In *Branzburg v. Hayes* (1972), the Supreme Court ruled that there is no First Amendment-based privilege that allows journalists to refuse to disclose evidence. The Court acknowledged that newsgathering is protected by the First Amendment, but ruled that forcing a journalist to reveal a source does not substantially interfere with a free press. After all, reporters may still collect information from legal sources and report their findings.

In *Branzburg,* a journalist had refused to identify persons he had seen using and selling drugs. Justice Byron R. White stated that the Court "cannot seriously entertain the notion that the First Amendment protects a newsman's agreement to conceal the criminal conduct of his source ... on the theory that it is better to write about crime than to do something about it."

Despite this ruling, a reporter may be held accountable for revealing a source's identity if the source was promised his or her identity would be kept secret. In *Cohen v. Cowles Media Co.* (1991), the *Minneapolis Star and Tribune* and the *St. Paul Pioneer Press Dispatch* printed information provided by a source after first promising the source that his identity would remain secret. However, both papers eventually revealed the source's identity. The source lost his job as a result of the papers' actions, and sued the publishers of both papers for breach of contract.

The publishers' argued that state officials cannot constitutionally punish a newspaper for printing truthful information about a public matter except in extraordinary circumstances. The Supreme Court, however, ruled that the papers were guilty of illegally breaching (breaking) their agreement with the source. The Court held that the press must follow laws (including contract laws) even if those laws might interfere with a paper's ability to gather information. For instance, the Court noted that the press may not break into an office to gather news. It was "beyond dispute" that the press has no "special immunity" from following general laws. Therefore, the First Amendment did not offer the press a constitutional right to disregard promises that would otherwise be enforceable under state law.

Freedom of Assembly and the Right to Petition the Government

The First Amendment guarantees individuals freedom of assembly (the right to meet or gather with others), and to petition (ask) the Government for a redress (correction) of grievances (complaints). People may petition the government in various manners, including sending written petitions (statements or requests) to government officials. For instance, between 1836 and 1840 more than two million people signed petitions opposing slavery. The petitions were sent to the U.S. House of Representatives in an effort to get Congress to make slavery illegal. Citizens may also petition the government by peacefully assembling in public places to call attention to political issues.

In *Edwards v. South Carolina* (1963), the Supreme Court overruled the conviction of 187 African American students who were arrested for demonstrating on the grounds of the state capitol in Columbia, South Carolina. The Court ruled that the convictions had infringed on the demonstrators' "rights of free speech, free assembly, and freedom to petition for redress of their grievances."

The First Amendment does not give demonstrators the right to break existing laws, or to prevent the proper use of public property. In *Adderly v. Florida* (1966), Harriet L. Adderly and other college students protested the arrest of civil rights protesters by blocking a jail driveway. When they ignored requests to leave the area, they were arrested and charged with trespass. The Supreme Court ruled that the state, like any private property owner, has the power to preserve its property "for the use to which it is lawfully dedicated."

And although citizens generally have the right demonstrate and assemble in public places, the government may regulate parades, processions, and large public gatherings by requiring a license for such activities. Licenses cannot, however, be granted or denied to a group because of its political message.

Who can you associate with?

The right to associate (join) with others is not specifically stated in the First Amendment, but courts have found that such a right is suggested by the guarantees of freedom of speech. The right to associate with people of one's choosing has allowed political parties and other politically active groups to form in the United states. But the freedom of political association is not absolute.

In *Scales v. United States* (1961), the Supreme Court upheld Section 2 of the Smith Act (see Freedom of Speech). This section made it a crime to belong to the Communist Party. The Court ruled that the provision applied only to "active" members of the Communist Party who had a "specific intent" to bring about the violent overthrow of the U.S. government.

The civil rights movement started in the 1950s, and led to attempts by some Southern state governments to suppress certain political activity. In *NAACP v. Alabama* (1958), the Supreme Court held that a state court's order violated a group's right to associate freely. The State of Alabama had requested the National Association for the Advancement of Colored People (NAACP) to disclose the names and addresses of its Alabama members. The Court ruled that the freedom to associate is inseparable from freedom of speech as long the association was not promoting illegal objectives. The Court stressed that the NAACP used only lawful means (such as boycotts) in seeking its goals.

FREEDOM TO DISASSOCIATE? Freedom of association includes the right *not* to associate with someone. For example, the government cannot force an

First Amendment

individual to support a certain belief or to join a particular political group. However, the Court has also ruled that the freedom of association does not include the right to discriminate against a person based on race, gender, or ethnic background.

In *Roberts v. United States Jaycees* (1984), the Court ruled that the Jaycees (a popular commercial association) could not deny admission to women simply because of their gender. The Court ruled that the government had a strong interest in eliminating sex discrimination, and assuring its citizens equal access to publicly available goods and services. Therefore, the government could force the Jaycees to allow women in their group.

A Statement of Principles

The First Amendment originally restricted the role the federal government could play in limiting free speech, political activities, and religious practices. Eventually, most of these limits were also applied to the activities of state and local governments. The free expression of ideas, however, has never been absolute. In the twentieth century, the growth of the mass media and new technologies led to renewed debates about the government's role in limiting free speech and a free press. Political and social protests led to arguments over the right to "peaceably assemble." And religious freedom issues were at the center of debate as courts struck down laws that gave government support to certain religious practices.

The Supreme Court has struggled to find a balance between the freedoms protected by the first amendment and other societal interests. As a result, the Court has relaxed some restrictions on free expression, and reinforced others. Even though the High Court's interpretation of the amendment has occasionally shifted, the Court has rarely wavered from the First Amendment's basic assertion that an individual's personal, religious, and political expression should be as free from government interference as possible.

For More Information

Books

Barron, Jerome A., and C. Thomas Dienes. *First Amendment Law in a Nutshell.* St. Paul, MN: West Publishing, 1993.

Guide to American Law. 12 vols. St. Paul, MN: West Publishing, 1987.

Hall, Kermit L. *The Magic Mirror.* New York: Oxford University Press, 1989.

Hickok, Jr., Eugene W., ed. *The Bill of Rights: Original Meaning and Current Understanding.* Charlottesville, VA: University Press of Virginia, 1991.

Oxford Companion to the Supreme Court of the United States. New York: Oxford University Press, 1992.

Stephens, Jr., Otis H., and John M. Scheb II. *American Constitutional Law.* St. Paul, MN: West Publishing, 1993.

CD-ROM

Encarta 1994 CD-ROM. Redmond, WA: Microsoft Corporation, 1994.

Encyclopedia Britannica 97 CD-ROM. Chicago, IL: Encyclopedia Brittanica, Inc., 1997.

**First
Amendment**

Second Amendment

A well-regulated militia, being necessary to the security of a free State, the right of the people to keep and bear Arms, shall not be infringed.

The Second Amendment contains two distinct phrases: It states that "the right of the people to keep and bear Arms shall not be infringed (limited)."

But is the right to keep and carry weapons an individual right? Or does the fact that the amendment seems to connect the right to bear arms to the necessity of keeping a "well-regulated militia" mean that the right of "the people" is actually the "collective right" of people to protect their communities with an armed local military force?

Whether the right to bear arms is an individual right or a collective right, whom specifically does the Second Amendment prohibit from infringing that right?

Those who believe it is a "collective" right argue that the Constitution gives control of the militia to the states and therefore the government of each state must have some power to regulate the purchase, possession, and use of firearms. According to this argument, the Second Amendment limits the federal government, not the states, from passing strict gun control laws. Supporters of gun control also argue that because the Second Amendment only protects the "collective right" to maintain a militia, the federal government may regulate individual ownership of guns without violating the amendment.

Opponents of gun control laws, or government interference with a person's ability to own guns, argue that the Second Amendment firmly establishes that the right to bear arms belongs to individual citizens and should not be infringed in any way by the federal government. They also argue that the Second Amendment should be applied equally to federal *and* state governments, in the same way other parts of the Bill of Rights are.

RATIFICATION FACTS

PROPOSED: Submitted by Congress to the states on September 25, 1789.

RATIFICATION: Ratified by the required three-fourths of states (eleven of fourteen) on December 15, 1791. Declared to be part of the Constitution on December 15, 1791.

RATIFYING STATES: Ratifying states: New Jersey, November 20, 1789; Maryland, December 19, 1789; North Carolina, December 22, 1789; South Carolina, January 19, 1790; New Hampshire, January 25, 1790; Delaware, January 28, 1790; New York, February 24, 1790; Pennsylvania, March 10, 1790; Rhode Island, June 7, 1790; Vermont, November 3, 1791; Virginia, December 15, 1791 (amendment adopted).

The prevalence of violent crime in the United States has sparked repeated public cries for stronger federal gun control laws. But such laws face equally vocal opposition from those who believe passionately in the individual's right to defend one's self and family. Indeed, Americans have a long tradition of gun ownership, dating to the first English settlements in North America.

Congress has passed very few laws limiting private gun ownership and as a result, only a handful of Second Amendment-related cases have come before the U.S. Supreme Court.

Origins of the Second Amendment

Private gun ownership has been a part of American culture since Great Britain sent settlers to North America in the early 1600s. From the beginning, it was British policy not only to allow its colonists to keep firearms but also to encourage them to do so, in order to protect themselves from Native Americans, French forces, and slave revolts. In fact, most colonies passed laws *requiring* male citizens to keep arms and to serve in the militia. As a result, militias staffed and controlled by colonists provided the bulk of the colonies' defenses for decades.

Second Amendment

The American Colonial Militia needed to keep arms in their homes because there was no organized, standing army.
Courtefy of the Library of Congress.

However, during the French and Indian War (1754–63), which pitted Britain against France and its Native American allies in North America, Great Britain sent its own soldiers to fight alongside colonial militias. The combined forces defeated France and established Britain as the dominant power in the northeast regions of North America.

The army moves in

When the war ended, Parliament decided to keep many of its soldiers in the colonies. The stated purpose of the peacetime army was to protect the colonies from Native American forces that were hostile to the colonies. Many colonists, however, believed the colonies could protect themselves. Furthermore, they feared the British troops were being kept in the colonies to keep the colonists in line. When Parliament passed the Quartering Act of 1765, which required the colonies to take responsibility for housing the British troops (see chapter three), many colonists were outraged over being forced to pay for the upkeep of an army they did not want.

Laws such as the Quartering Act and the Townsend Act (1767), which placed a tariff (tax) on goods shipped into the colonies, caused a great deal of unrest. Colonists were particularly upset because Parliament

was passing laws that directly affected the colonies, even though the colonies were not allowed to elect representatives to Parliament. "No taxation without representation," became a popular cry in the colonies as tension over British policies grew.

On March 5, 1770, British soldiers who had been sent to keep order fired into an angry, but unarmed, crowd of colonists in the city of Boston, killing five men. Public outcry over the incident, which became known as the Boston Massacre, led to even greater anti-British sentiment in the colonies.

Taking arms against the army

Conflict between the colonies and Parliament continued, and a new wave of tariffs prompted the colonies to create the First Continental Congress in June 1774. Delegates to the assembly passed a point-by-point condemnation of Parliament's actions in the colonies and called on the colonies to arm themselves in defense against the British Army. In fact, the colonies continued to maintain militias, despite the presence of British troops, and the American population remained heavily armed. It was a British decision to disarm the Americans, however, that led to the first shots of the Revolutionary War (1775–1783), in which the American colonies won their independence.

On April 18, 1775, British troops were sent to disarm a militia force just outside of Boston. The British soldiers met seventy of the Massachusetts Patriots (as the militiamen called themselves) in the town of Lexington. During an argument between the two groups a shot was fired, leading to the first exchange of firepower in the American Revolution.

In the wake of the battle, British General Thomas Gage, (1721–1787), who was stationed in Boston, took more steps to disarm the colonists in the area. Gage promised he would allow people who turned in their firearms to leave the city safely. After the skirmishes with British soldiers, many Bostonians were afraid of staying in the city and quickly accepted the general's offer. Once they turned in their arms, however, Gage refused to allow them to leave. Soon after, word spread that the British intended to disarm all Americans and make it a crime for any colonist to bear arms.

The threat of disarmament by British forces (who had already proved themselves capable of violence against the colonists) helped spark all-out war between Britain and the colonies. To better wage war

Second Amendment

The American Revolution found the colonies pulling together to fight against the British.

with the British, the colonies eventually established the Continental Army, under the leadership of General George Washington (1732–1799), who later became the first president of the United States. America's well-armed population, fighting in militias and in the new Continental Army, ultimately defeated the larger, more experienced British forces in 1781 (see Introduction).

A Constitutional Right to Bear Arms

Initially, the newly independent states formed a loose union under the Articles of Confederation (1781). Under the terms of this agreement, the state governments gave up very little of their power to the new federal (or national) government. In 1787, delegates from twelve of the thirteen states crafted a new constitution that granted the federal government considerably more power than it had under the Articles of Confederation.

The new constitution divided the national government into three powerful branches: the executive branch, led by a powerful president; the judicial branch, led by the Supreme Court (see below), and Congress (the

legislative or lawmaking body of government). Under the proposed constitution, the new Congress would have the power to impose taxes, regulate interstate trade, declare war, and raise an army. In addition, Congress could call on the state militias to aid in the defense of the nation.

Before the new constitution could go into effect, however, it had to be ratified (agreed to) by three-quarters of the states. Many people worried that the new government would be too powerful. It was eventually agreed that after the new constitution was ratified, Congress would add a number of amendments (corrections or additions) to it detailing the rights of the states and the people.

The memory of the British government's attempt to disarm the militia was still strong in America. The Constitution (which was ratified in 1788) gave states the power to maintain militias, but many of those who opposed it wanted an amendment that specifically gave states the power to maintain a militia and citizens the right to bear arms.

During the first term of Congress (1789–1791), Virginia statesman James Madison (1751–1836), who later became the fourth president of the United States, wrote a number of proposals for amendments to the Constitution. These included a proposal for what became the Second Amendment. Borrowing from various state constitutions, Madison's proposal stated, in part, that "A well-regulated militia, composed of the body of the people, being the best security of a free state, the right of the people to keep and bear arms shall not be infringed . . .."

The Senate removed a clause that gave people the right to avoid militia service on religious grounds (see chapter one). It also replaced the words "being the best security" with "being necessary to the security" and removed the phrase "composed of the body of the people." The final version was sent to the states for ratification on September 25, 1789, and was officially adopted, as one of the first ten amendments, or Bill of Rights, on December 15, 1791.

Whose right is it anyway?

During the American Revolution, colonies began rewriting their charters to form state constitutions. Many of these constitutions specifically ensured the right to keep and bear arms. The Virginia Declaration of Rights, written in 1776, declared "That a well-regulated Militia, composed of the body of the people, trained to arms, is the proper, natural, and safe defence (sic) of a free State." The same year, Pennsylvania's constitution proclaimed "That the people have a right to bear arms for the

defense of themselves and the state." In 1780, the Massachusetts Declaration of Rights stated that "The people have a right to keep and bear arms for the common defense."

The Pennsylvania constitution specifically mentions the people's right to bear arms to defend *themselves*, but the Virginia and Massachusetts declarations only mention the need for a "common" or statewide defense. Although members of Congress certainly would have been aware of Pennsylvania's constitution, the Second Amendment only mentions the defense of the state in its guarantee of the right to bear arms. This would seem to indicate that the Second Amendment was only intended to protect the right to bear arms to the extent that it was necessary for the upkeep of state militias.

More specific wording would likely have limited debate on the subject. In *Bliss v. Kentucky* (1822), for instance, the Kentucky Supreme Court struck down a state law that prohibited the carrying of concealed weapons by citing Kentucky's constitutional guarantee of "the right of citizens to bear arms in defense of *themselves* and the state." (Emphasis added.) The court considered the right to bear arms as both a collective and individual right, and ruled that individuals had an unlimited right to bear arms.

Regular Joes or GI Joes? The Changing Role of America's Militia

In examining the different interpretations of the Second Amendment, it is useful to consider the changing relationship between the militia and the individual citizen. At the time the Second Amendment was written, one could argue that there was very little practical difference between an individual right to bear arms and a collective right to maintain a militia. That was because members of the militia were not full-time soldiers. They were regular members of the community — farmers, butchers, lawyers — called to duty in times of emergency. Furthermore, these citizens were responsible for keeping and maintaining their own weapons. In other words, it was impossible to have a well-armed militia unless individual citizens were also well armed.

However, during the American Revolutionary War, militias made up of ordinary citizens were often under trained and undisciplined. In 1776, George Washington warned the Continental Congress that relying on the state militias to fight Britain was like "resting upon a broken staff." While the presence of a well-armed citizenry played an important role in the ability of the colonies to defeat the British Army, it was the creation of the Continental Army, with full-time professional soldiers, that turned the tide of the war in the Americans' favor. Nonetheless, after the war, Congress immediately reduced the Continental Army to eighty men. This meant responsibility for the defense of the nation was, for the most part, returned to the state militias.

A nation of soldiers

Recognizing how weak the existing militia system was, Henry Knox (1750–1806), who served as U.S. secretary of war from 1785 to 1794, tried to convince Congress to take measures to create a nation of true citizen soldiers. Knox and others believed that a nation in which every citizen was ready and able to take up arms in the country's defense would have little need for an army of full-time professional soldiers. Furthermore, supporters of a strong militia argued that people who participated in the nation's defense as members of the militia would become more responsible citizens.

Prominent leaders from Washington to Madison and Thomas Jefferson (1743–1826) supported Knox's ideas. Congress passed the Militia Act of 1792, which required every able-bodied male between the ages of eighteen and forty-five to participate in the militia and to provide for their own equipment at their own expense. This act would seem to support the argument that the collective right to bear arms required that individuals (at least all men between eighteen and forty-five) also have the right to bear arms.

Return of the "broken staff"

THE WAR OF 1812. The Militia Act of 1792 did little to improve the quality of the militia. It contained no requirements for militia training, and the militia remained an unruly, poorly equipped force. Congress called on the state militias to defend the country from British invasion during the War of 1812 (1812–15). Almost 400,000 of the militiamen called to battle during the war refused to serve beyond the end of their required six-month terms. During the war, which ended indecisively, the American forces suffered a number of embarrassments, including the British capture of Washington, D.C. The war led to a call for better militia training, but Congress did little to change the system.

THE CIVIL WAR. The American Civil War (1861–65) pitted the Northern States (the Union) against the Southern States (the Confederates) in a

lengthy and bloody battle over states' rights, federal power, and slavery. During the war, militia units on both sides of the conflict often left as soon as their term of service was over. At the First Battle of Bull Run, militiamen withdrew from the Union forces in mid-battle because their term of service had ended.

As in the Revolutionary War, it was not until men began to volunteer for duty that the quality of tactics and training improved. But again, with the end of the war, Congress quickly reduced the size of the army and returned responsibility for defending the country to state militias.

THE SPANISH-AMERICAN WAR. At the end of the nineteenth century, state militias were called on once again to fight, and once again there were problems. The Spanish-American War (1898) was fought largely in Cuba, Puerto Rico, and the Philippines, and some militia units refused to go, claiming such affairs were outside the responsibility of the militia. The militia units fought beside regiments of volunteers (who were not under the authority of the states) and America eventually emerged victorious. But the war highlighted, again, the danger of relying on poorly trained, ill-equipped state militias for national defense.

In his first annual message to Congress, on December 3, 1901, President Theodore Roosevelt (1858–1919), who had fought in the Spanish-American War, said, "Our militia law is obsolete and worthless. The organization and armament of the National Guard of the several States ... should be made identical with those provided for the regular forces."

Roosevelt's secretary of war, Elihu Root (1845–1937), told Congress in 1902, "It is really absurd that a nation which maintains but a small Regular Army and depends upon unprofessional citizen soldiery for its defense should run along as we have done for over one hundred and ten years under a militia law which never worked satisfactorily in the beginning, and which was perfectly obsolete before any man now fit for military duty was born. The result is that we have practically no militia system."

Nationalizing the guard

Between 1901 and 1903, Congress enacted three laws, sometimes referred to jointly as the Dick Act, which had the effect of turning the army into a modern fighting force. These laws included the 1903 Militia Act, which required the National Guard to conform to the organization of the regular army and required Congress to pay for the Guard's equipment. Furthermore, the militia was to be trained by officers of the army.

These new statutes marked the end of militias made up of armed ordinary citizens as set up by the Militia Act of 1792. With the federal government taking primary responsibility for arming and training the state military forces, it was no longer clear that a state's ability to maintain a strong militia depends on the right of individuals to keep and bear arms.

Some argue that these changes erase any argument for banning federal regulation of the right to bear arms. Others argue that Second Amendment was designed specifically to protect the states from federal interference, and therefore the federal government should never be allowed to interfere with the states' ability to establish the right to bear arms within their borders. Other opponents of gun control argue that the Second Amendment was designed to protect an individual's right to bear arms—regardless of the state's needs.

Sawed-off Shotguns, Tommy Guns, and the Supreme Court

In the case of *United States v. Miller* (1939) the Supreme Court considered all of these arguments. The ruling in *Miller* touched on the government's ability to regulate firearms; the historical evolution of the concept of militia as it pertains to and limits the individual rights guaranteed by the Second Amendment; and the individual right to bear arms embodied in the Second Amendment.

The Constitution of the United States establishes the Supreme Court as the nation's highest court. It is responsible for the final interpretation of laws (including amendments to the Constitution) in the United States. Originally consisting of six justices (judges), the Supreme Court was expanded to include nine justices in 1869. In deciding cases, justices may write individual opinions (explaining the legal reasoning behind the justice's vote) or sign another justice's opinion. The court's final ruling in a case is based on a simple vote of all nine justices.

The first federal gun control act

Violent crime and the growing influence of organized crime in the 1920s and 1930s prompted Congress to pass the National Firearms Act of 1934 in an effort to strengthen law enforcement's powers. The act was the federal government's first statute to regulate the sale and use of firearms. The law set an enormous tax on automatic weapons (such as machine guns or "tommy guns") and sawed-off shotguns that were trans-

Second Amendment

ported across state borders and also required that the weapons be registered. Until this time, regulation of firearms was left solely to state and local authorities. Congress believed that the commerce clause of the Constitution (Article 1, Section 8, Clause 3), gave it the power to regulate interstate transportation of weapons. The commerce clause states that Congress has the power "to regulate Commerce with foreign nations, among the several States, and with the Indian Tribes."

The defendants in *United States v. Miller* were Jack Miller and Frank Layton. The two men were indicted in Arkansas for violation of the National Firearms Act of 1934 because they had transported an unregistered sawed-off shotgun from Oklahoma to Arkansas. The defendants challenged the National Firearms Act, arguing in part that the law violated their Second Amendment right to bear arms.

The U.S. Supreme Court unanimously upheld the constitutionality of the National Firearms Act of 1934. With regard to the Second Amendment, the court ruled that the amendment applied only to the actions of the federal government. According to the decision, nothing in the Second Amendment prevents state and local governments from pass-

The fact that gun ownership has become so widespread has led to the tightening of security in many public places such as schools and airports.

Reproduced by permission of Corbis-Bettmann.

ing gun control laws. The Court went on to state that the Second Amendment guarantees were written into the Bill of Rights with the "obvious purpose to assure the continuation and render possible the effectiveness of the militias."

The Court concluded that, "In the absence of any evidence tending to show that possession of a [firearm] . . . has some reasonable relationship to the preservation or efficiency of well regulated militia, we cannot say that the Second Amendment guarantees the right to keep and bear such an instrument. Certainly it is not within judicial notice that [the weapon in this case] is any part of the ordinary military equipment or that its use could contribute to the common defense.

Because *Miller* is the only Supreme Court case that directly addresses the main issues surrounding the Second Amendment, it has been the focal point of the current gun control debate. Interestingly, both sides use *Miller* to argue their case.

Those who favor gun control say the court ruled definitively that the right to bear arms is not an individual right, but rather a collective right held by members of the militias of the states, or National Guard.

Individual rights advocates argue that the wording of the *Miller* decision indicates that individuals in the states should be allowed to keep and bear arms, as long as they are like those used by the National Guard and the armed services.

Further Rulings

After *Miller,* the issue of gun control largely disappeared, until the 1960s. With violent crime once again on the rise, Congress began enacting a series of strict laws in 1968, using the commerce clause to control interstate sale and registration of firearms and ammunition and generally avoiding Second Amendment challenges.

Meanwhile, several lower court decisions in the 1960s and 1970s continued to uphold the states' right to regulate firearms. The courts maintained the position that the Second Amendment in no way prevents states from restricting the sale, possession, maintenance, or ownership of firearms. These cases bolstered the argument that the guarantee of the right to bear arms was intended as a collective right, not an individual right.

In *Burton v. Sills* (1968), the New Jersey Supreme Court reviewed a Second Amendment challenge to a New Jersey gun control statute. The

Second Amendment

Many guns that should only be used in the armed forces as a part of war are confiscated on the streets of America every day.

Reproduced by permission of AP/Wide World Photos.

decision in the case is consistent with lower federal court and state court opinions that have continually interpreted the Second Amendment right to bear arms as "framed in contemplation not of individual rights but of the maintenance of the states' active, organized militias."

The decision further stated that the Second Amendment "is not designed to secure personal liberties against intrusion by government but to protect one governmental unit, the state, against subjection by another unit, the Federal government."

The Brady Bill, a federal law passed in 1994, imposes a list of requirements for handgun ownership. The bill was championed by James Brady, a White House press secretary who was crippled by a bullet during a failed attempt to assassinate President Ronald Reagan in 1981.

Other major legislation, including the Violent Crime Control & Law Enforcement Act of 1993, followed in the wake of several incidents where such weapons were used against unarmed adults and children, and against officers of the federal government.

To date, no federal court has struck down such federal gun control legislation as a violation of the Second Amendment. However, in *United States v. Lopez* (1995) the Supreme Court ruled that Congress had gone too far in using the commerce clause to pass the Gun-Free School Zones Act of 1990. The act sought to control firearms and curtail armed violence in and around schools. Congress used its commerce clause powers to ban any individual from possessing "a firearm at a place that [he] knows . . . is a school zone." The Supreme Court ruled that the act "had nothing to do with commerce or any sort of economic enterprise" and therefore was outside of Congress's power to enforce. Any such restrictions on guns in school zones therefore were left to the states.

What the Feds Can't Do, the States Can

The states have always had greater power to regulate the use of arms than the federal government. That is because the Bill of Rights was originally only intended to limit the powers of the newly formed federal government. The states, meanwhile, were free to operate under the rules of their own constitutions. For instance, the governments of Connecticut and Massachusetts ran state-supported Congregational churches into the 1800s, despite the First Amendment's ban on government-sponsored religions (see chapter one).

Second Amendment

In the case of *Barron v. Mayor & City Council of Baltimore* (1833), a citizen sued the city of Baltimore under the Fifth Amendment's just compensation clause (see chapter five) after the city took actions that made the citizen's business virtually worthless. The just compensation clause requires the government to pay a fair price for any private property it seizes or destroys for public use.

However, in a unanimous decision, the Supreme Court ruled that the Bill of Rights could only be applied to the federal government. The Court stated that "Each State established a constitution for itself, and in that constitution provided such limitations and restrictions on the powers of its particular government as its judgment dictated." Furthermore, the limitations on power put on the government of the United States by its Constitution were "naturally and necessarily applicable (only) to the government" created by that Constitution — namely the federal government.

Applying the Bill of Rights to state governments

In the wake of the Civil War, many southern states enacted a series of laws geared to limiting the civil rights of African Americans

Guns used by hunters are regulated, and a hunter must obtain a special gun permit to own one. Reproduced by permission of AP/Wide World Photos.

who had been freed from slavery during the war. Among the many restrictions put into effect by these so-called Black Codes were laws barring former slaves from owning firearms or restricting their use. Ratification of the Fourteenth Amendment in 1868 stemmed directly from such abusive laws.

The Fourteenth Amendment's due process and equal protection clauses (see chapter fourteen) required states to protect "life, liberty, and property" with due process, that is, with fair and equal application of the law. Eventually this clause changed the way the Supreme Court applied the Bill of Rights. The Court has used the due process and equal protection clauses to apply different parts of the Bill of Rights to state and local governments, as well as the federal government.

However, the Second Amendment is one of three amendments in the Bill of Rights (together with the Third and Seventh) that the Supreme Court has never applied to the states by in "incorporating" it with the requirements of the Fourteenth Amendment.

In *Presser v. Illinois* (1886), the Supreme Court upheld an Illinois law that prohibited any group other than the regular organized volunteer militia of the state to drill or parade with arms. The Court unanimously held that the Second Amendment applied only to acts of the federal government, and did not prevent the state from restricting association in a paramilitary organization or regulating or prohibiting drilling or parading with arms.

In *Quilici v. Village of Morton Grove* (1982) a U.S. appeals court decision let stand a local ordinance passed by the village of Morton Grove, Illinois, which banned the possession of handguns in the home. Handgun owners in the village were required to turn in their guns to the local police department and store guns for recreational use at gun clubs and gun ranges. In refusing to strike down the law, the appeals court ruled that the Second Amendment does not apply to the states and local governments. By refusing to hear the case itself, the Supreme Court also refused to apply the Second Amendment to the states.

Those who argue that individuals have a natural right to bear arms for self-defense argue that the Supreme Court should incorporate the Second Amendment in its application of the Fourteenth Amendment just as it has incorporated other Bill of Rights amendments. But at this date, state governments may regulate an individual's ability to keep and bear arms within the state's boundaries, and most states regulate gun ownership in some capacity.

Second Amendment

The Branch Davidians were so heavily armed that special government forces had to be called in to confront them. The resulting gun battle and a fire killed many of the people belonging to the para-military religious sect.

A NEW MILITIA? The term militia has taken on new meanings since the 1980s. Heavily armed private military groups, not associated with state or federal government, have claimed Second Amendment rights as militiamen under the militia clause of the amendment. However, the courts have not accepted this claim, and the ruling in *Presser v. Illinois* (1886), which emphatically gave states the power to regulate such groups, has not been reversed by any more recent Supreme Court decisions.

The Battle Continues

A general review of the court cases dealing with the Second Amendment suggests that the courts have so far upheld the collective right definition of the amendment's "right to keep and bear arms." In addition, the courts have clearly indicated the government's right to regulate state militias and their operation.

Furthermore, the Supreme Court has routinely ruled that the states have the power to regulate arms without regard to the Second Amendment. The Second Amendment has never been incorporated under the Fourteenth Amendment. Although there have been several attempts

*The ease with which
some people are
obtaining guns has
had some deadly
consequences and
has left some people
questioning the
validity of the right
to bear arms. This is
the aftermath of the
Colombine High
School shooting.*

Second Amendment

to pass gun control laws at the federal level, most laws regulating the right to bear arms exist at the state level.

The judicial and legislative history has clearly shown that both the federal and state governments have the right to regulate firearms and may prohibit some categories of arms altogether, such as automatic assault weapons, machine guns, and sawed-off shotguns. However, America's historical tradition of private gun ownership has led to the creation of a powerful gun-rights groups that actively opposes national gun control. And in light of the few Supreme Court cases that address the Second Amendment directly, it is likely that the battle over gun control will continue to take place primarily at the state level.

For More Information

Books

Arsenault, Raymond, ed. *Crucible of Liberty: 200 Years of the Bill of Rights.* New York: Free Press/Macmillan, 1991.

Cottrol, Robert J., ed. *Gun Control and the Constitution: Sources and Explorations on the Second Amendment.* New York: Garland Publishing, 1994.

Cramer, Clayton E. *For the Defense of Themselves and the State: The Original Intent and Judicial Interpretation of the Right to Keep and Bear Arms.* Westport, Conn.: Praeger Publishers, 1994.

Cress, Lawrence Delbert. *Citizens in Arms: The Army and Militia in American Society to the War of 1812.* Chapel Hill: University of North Carolina Press, 1982.

Cunliffe, Marcus. *Soldiers and Civilians: The Martial Spirit of America 1775–1865.* Boston: Little, Brown & Co., 1968.

Edel, Wilbur. *Gun Control: Threat to Liberty or Defense Against Anarchy?* Westport, Conn.: Praeger Publishers, 1995.

Encyclopedia of World Biography. 17 vols. Detroit: Gale Research, 1998.

Freedman, Warren. *The Privilege to Keep and Bear Arms: The Second Amendment and Its Interpretation.* Westport, Conn.: Quorum Books, 1989.

Halbrook, Stephen P. *A Right to Bear Arms: State and Federal Bills of Rights and Constitutional Guarantees.* Albuquerque: University of New Mexico Press, 1984.

—. *That Every Man Be Armed: The Evolution of a Constitutional Right.* Albuquerque: University of New Mexico Press, 1984.

Hamilton, Neil A. *Militias in America: A Reference Handbook.* Santa Barbara, Calif.: ABC-CLIO, 1996.

Kohn, Richard H. *Eagle and Sword: The Beginnings of the Military Establishment in America.* Free Press/Macmillan, 1975.

Kruschke, Earl R. *Gun Control: A Reference Handbook.* Santa Barbara, Calif.: ABC-CLIO, 1995.

Mahon, John K. *History of the Militia and the National Guard.* New York: Macmillan Publishing Co., 1983.

Malcolm, Joyce Lee. *To Keep and Bear Arms: The Origins of the Anglo-American Right.* Cambridge, Mass.: Harvard University Press, 1994.

Millett, Allan R., and Peter Maslowski. *For the Common Defense: A Military History of the United States of America.* New York: Free Press/Macmillan, 1984.

Riker, William H. *Soldiers of the States: The Role of the National Guard in American Democracy.* Washington, D.C.: Public Affairs Press, 1957.

Articles
Wiener, Frederick. "The Militia Clause of the Constitution." *Harvard Law Review* 54 (1940): 181–220.

Second Amendment

Third Amendment

No Soldier shall, in time of peace be quartered in any house, without the consent of the Owner, nor in time of war, but in a manner to be prescribed by law.

Quartering (or billeting) is the practice of housing soldiers in homes or buildings intended for other purposes (such as town halls or court houses). The Third Amendment prohibits the government from forcing anyone to quarter soldiers in any house during times of peace, although building owners may agree to quarter troops just as they might rent to any person.

The Third Amendment also bans forced quartering during times of war, unless a law specifically allowing wartime quartering is passed. By requiring a law to allow quartering, the amendment guarantees that only Congress, the legislative (law making) body of the United States government, can pave the way for the quartering of troops, and then only during a war.

Since its adoption the Third Amendment has not been the subject of much controversy. Unlike the First and Second Amendments, for example, the Third Amendment has rarely been the subject of court cases, protests, or political debates.

Despite its quiet role in the history of the independent United States, the quartering of soldiers was one of the key issues leading to the American Revolutionary War (1775–83), in which the American colonies fought for independence from Great Britain.

Why Was Quartering an Issue?

Having soldiers living in your house may seem like a preposterous idea now. American sailors, soldiers, and airmen usually live on military bases, aboard ships, or in their own homes. In the years before America

RATIFICATION FACTS

PROPOSED: Submitted by Congress to the states on September 25, 1789 along with the other nine amendments that comprise the Bill of Rights.

RATIFICATION: The amendment was ratified on December 15, 1791, when Virginia became the eleventh of the fourteen states in existence to ratify. The remaining three states, Massachusetts, Georgia, and Connecticut all ratified the amendment in the spring of 1939.

RATIFYING STATES: New Jersey, November 20, 1789; Maryland, December 19, 1789; North Carolina, December 22, 1789; South Carolina, January 19, 1790; New Hampshire, January 25, 1790; Delaware, January 28, 1790; New York, February 24, 1790; Pennsylvania, March 10, 1790; Rhode Island, June 7, 1790; Vermont, November 3, 1791; Virginia, December 15, 1791 (amendment adopted).

won its independence, however, the British government occasionally required Americans to lodge soldiers in private houses or buildings when the army did not have adequate barracks (military living quarters).

British troops in North America (called Redcoats, because of their bright red uniform jackets) were mostly soldiers from England, Scotland, and Ireland. These troops were often moved from one part of Great Britain's American colonies to another depending on where they were needed. This constant movement would occasionally leave the soldiers without barracks or necessary supplies. At such times, the army could require local citizens to house soldiers or provide supplies.

But the British government was also known to have quartered soldiers in places where there were signs of unrest among the people. Having armed troops living among the people was seen as a way for the government to keep potential troublemakers in line. During America's colonial years, Britain required colonists to quarter troops for both reasons.

The Wild West and Wartime Quartering

The issue of quartering troops first arose in the American colonies during the French and Indian War (1754–63). By the middle of the sixteenth

**Third
Amendment**

century, most of the northeast and mid-west section of North America was under the control of Great Britain and France. (Spain still controlled territories in some western and southern parts of the continent.) The French and Indian War pitted the British against the French for domination of the continent. Several Native American tribes also fought on the side of France, which was considered friendlier to Native American interests than Britain.

Many people in Britain's American colonies welcomed the war. The colonists did not like having the French army in nearby Canada and in the territories just west of colonies. In fact, many colonists hoped to claim land in these largely unsettled territories controlled by France and Native Americans (see "A Revolutionary Training Ground" box).

During the war, the commander of the British Army in North America, Lord Loudoun, ordered colonists to quarter British troops when necessary. As a result, soldiers were housed in both public buildings and private houses when barracks were unavailable.

Loudoun's orders did not require the British government to pay owners for the cost of quartering troops in their buildings. Instead, the responsibility was passed to the colonial legislatures (the law-making institutions of the individual colonies).

Colonial legislatures could only raise money by taxing colonists. This meant the cost of keeping British troops in American houses was actually being passed back to the colonists themselves. Though many Americans were glad to have the protection of the British troops, some were angered by the new policies. Americans had paid almost no taxes to Great Britain before and were not happy about paying, even indirectly, for the activities of the British army.

In the summer of 1756 major protests against the quartering orders took place in Albany, New York (a significant center of military operations during the war). In response to these protests, Loudoun sent a brigade of armed soldiers to the city and seized, among other buildings, a church for gunpowder storage. This use of private property for military purposes only increased the protesters' anger.

Sowing the Seeds of Discontent

By the end of the French and Indian War in 1763, Great Britain was deeply in debt. The British had spent enormous amounts of money ousting the French from North America and were determined to keep a large

*This is the actual
Stamp Act stamp
as it would appear
on a newspaper or
legal document.*
Courtesy of the Library
of Congress.

army on the continent to protect their new territories. Such permanent armies are called standing armies.

In 1765 the British Parliament (the legislative branch of the British government) passed two acts to help offset the cost of maintaining its forces in America. The Stamp Act required that most paper goods, such as newspapers and legal documents, had to bear a tax stamp, which had to be purchased from the government. The Quartering Act—sometimes called the First Quartering Act—required colonial legislatures to pay the costs of housing British troops and to

provide them with supplies. Though the act did not allow for quartering in people's homes, many people resented any provision for quartering troops in time of peace.

Stomping the Stamp Act

Not only were the colonists not used to paying taxes to Britain, many of them felt that Parliament had no right to tax the colonies since there were no American representatives in Parliament. This concept of "no taxation without representation" became one of the major issues in America's independence movement.

Colonists protested the Stamp Act in pamphlets and speeches and in organized demonstrations. There were also riots in which colonists attacked the homes of the men who were to be in charge of selling the stamps. American outrage over the new tax forced the British to revoke the Stamp Act before it ever took effect.

All the king's men or all the king's goons?

The decision to keep a standing army in the colonies was very unpopular with the colonists. Some saw the army's very presence during peacetime as a violation of the colonists' rights as free people. (Even in England, citizens often argued against keeping a large army in times of peace.)

The colonies had already had their share of arguments with the British government, especially since King George III had come to power in 1760. The colonists felt that Parliament had become less responsive to their concerns during George's reign and worried that the British army would be used to enforce British policies in America.

The Quartering Act was passed to help offset the cost of maintaining these troops. But the British also hoped that housing troops among the colonists would quiet colonial protesters. Instead it had the opposite effect. Many colonists were outraged by the Quartering Act and feared that it would lead to martial law (rule by the military). This anger turned into open protest across the colonies.

In August of 1766 the New York legislative assembly refused to comply with the new laws. Under the threat of armed force the assembly eventually backed down and agreed to abide by the Quartering Act. But within the colonies the seed of revolution had been planted.

English Roots of American Anti-Quartering Sentiment

Many of the rights colonists were demanding in America were rights that English citizens had already won. What bothered many Americans was not that Britain ruled the colonies, but that it did not rule the colonies in the same way it ruled England.

In England laws prohibited the quartering of troops in private homes without the consent of the owner. In a 1603 court case known as *Semayne's Case,* the English court found that "The house of every one is to him as his castle and fortress, as well for his defense against injury and violence, as for his repose." It is believed that this quote is where the saying "a man's home is his castle" came from.

Statute regulates quartering

The English Bill of Rights also regulated quartering. Passed in Parliament in 1689, the statute outlined the nature of the English government. Among its provisions was a stipulation that prohibited the government from quartering troops in private homes. Though it did not ban quartering troops in other establishments, such as inns or warehouses, the English Bill of Rights required the government to pay rent to those whose property was used for lodging troops.

Benjamin Franklin defends American rights

The fact that English citizens were protected from the very billeting of soldiers that the colonists were being forced to endure infuriated Americans. Less than two months after the First Quartering Act went into effect, Benjamin Franklin (1706–1790) wrote an essay in defense of American rights.

The essay was published in the English newspaper *The Gazeteer and New Daily Advertiser* on May 2, 1765. Franklin, who was an American representative to England at the time, wrote, "Let [the English], first try the effects of quartering soldiers on butchers, bakers, or other private houses [in England], and then transport the measure to America.... The people of England and America are the same; one King, and one law; and those who endeavour to promote a distinction, are truly enemies to both."

Though some colonists were already talking about independence from Great Britain, Franklin's call for equal treatment was based on the idea that the colonies were part of the British Empire, and should be treated as such.

**Third
Amendment**

Parliament members support Franklin

Some members of Parliament, including William Pitt (1708–1778), agreed with Franklin. In 1766 Pitt argued, "The poorest man may in his cottage bid defiance to all forces of the Crown. It may be frail—its roof may shake—the wind may blow through it—the storm may enter—the rain may enter—but the King of England cannot enter—all his force dares not cross the threshold of the ruined tenement!"

Pitt's argument for freedom from government interference within all British subjects' homes, however, did not sway Parliament to change its policies in the colonies.

Marching Toward the Inevitable

Still desperate for money, the British passed the Townsend Acts (1767), which placed a duty (tax) on a number of goods that the Americans shipped into the colonies, including glass, paper, and tea. These duties did raise some money for the government but barely put a dent in the cost of keeping an army in the colonies.

Great Britain began moving troops from expensive outposts in the western territories back to the populous cities in the east. This was done partially to save money. But after several years of American protests, Parliament was convinced that something had to be done to keep order in the colonies.

A soldier in every home?

In 1768 the British sent several thousand troops to Boston, Massachusetts. Massachusetts had been a center of American protests and the site of some of the most violent rioting. The troops were sent to the city to keep order and make sure the Townsend duties were paid on goods shipped into Boston Harbor.

The people of Massachusetts argued that the soldiers should stay in the barracks on Castle Island in Boston Harbor. This was where British troops had been housed in the past. The British force, however, was determined to make its presence felt in the city. British soldiers refused to stay on Castle Island. Instead they camped in the Boston Common, a public park in the middle of the city, and took lodging in the town hall and several other buildings (for which they did pay rent).

Despite the occupation of Boston, the Massachusetts council continued to openly defy the Quartering Act, refusing to supply or house the troops whenever possible. Tensions in the city led to regular clashes

Crispus Attucks became a famous casualty of the Boston Massacre. Courtesy of the Library of Congress.

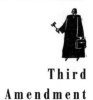
between Bostonians and the British troops.

Redcoats spill American blood

On March 5, 1770, a group of British soldiers and a crowd of Boston residents became entangled in a loud conflict. The crowd taunted the soldiers, yelling insults and hurling snowballs and rocks at them. The soldiers apparently felt threatened and fired into the unarmed crowd, killing five Americans (see "Crispus Attucks" box).

Colonists dubbed the incident the Boston Massacre, and the shootings became a rallying point for anti-British colonists. Dr. Joseph Warren, a resident of Boston at the time, wrote that such violence was to be expected "when the troops are informed that the intention of their being stationed in any city is to overawe [intimidate] the inhabitants."

Writing about the Boston Massacre, John Adams (1735–1826), who became the second President of the United States, wrote that "on that night the foundation of American Independence was laid." The soldiers accused of shooting the Americans were all found innocent or let go with a small punishment. But anger over the killings grew, and the British soon moved their troops out of Boston to Castle Island. Parliament also canceled most of the duties imposed by the Townsend Act. But a tax on tea was left in place to make it clear to Americans that Parliament still had the power to impose laws and levy taxes on the colonies.

**Third
Amendment**

Going overboard?

In 1773 Parliament used its power to give the British merchant company known as the East India Company the exclusive right to sell tea in America. This act also met with protest in the colonies. When three East India Company ships docked in Boston Harbor, a group of colonists thought to be led by pro-independence leader Samuel Adams (1722–1803), disguised themselves as Native Americans, boarded the ships, and threw the tea overboard.

The "Boston Tea Party" was a turning point in the relationship between Great Britain and the American colonies. Angered by this rebellious act of vandalism, Parliament passed the Coercive Acts (1774), designed to punish Massachusetts. Among other things, the acts, which colonists called the "Intolerable Acts," closed the Boston Harbor (until the destroyed tea was paid for) and replaced the elected Massachusetts Council with a council appointed by the governor.

Parliament strikes back

The "Intolerable Acts" also included a new Quartering Act that expanded the earlier Quartering Act to include quartering soldiers in pri-

and throwing snowballs at the troops, Attucks is said to have yelled, "They dare not fire." But after being knocked down, one soldier fired above the crowd and seconds later other soldiers began firing into the crowd.

Attucks was hit twice in the chest and died on the spot. In all, five colonists were killed, including Attucks, James Caldwell, Samuel Maverick, Patrick Carr and Samuel Gray. What began as a fight between two individuals turned into the first full-blown confrontation between British soldiers and anti-British colonists.

A trial found that the soldiers had acted in self-defense. Public opinion in the colonies, however, condemned the men as killers. Anti-British colonists labeled the incident the Boston Massacre and celebrated the slain men as martyrs. Historians debate whether the men were heroes or unruly members of a lawless mob. But it is undeniable that their defiant attitude and violent deaths helped fuel the call for American independence.

vate homes. General Thomas Gage, the commander of the British army in America at the time, was also appointed governor of Massachusetts, which effectively put the state under military rule.

In response to these actions, the colonies formed the First Continental Congress, which included representatives from twelve of the American colonies. Meeting in October 1774, the Continental Congress agreed on a *Declaration and Resolves.* This document outlined the colonial stand on a number of issues. On the subject of quartering troops, the document declared that "the keeping of a standing army in these colonies, in times of peace, without the consent of the legislature of that colony, in which such army is kept, is against the law."

Quartering and the Declaration of Independence

The American Revolutionary War began in 1775, less than a year after the Coercive Acts were passed. There were, of course, many reasons for the final outbreak of war between the colonies and Great Britain. But the quartering of troops played a large part in swaying American public opinion in favor of the fight for independence.

Third
Amendment

*Paul Revere etched
this picture of the
Boston Massacre.*
Courtesy of the Library
of Congress.

In the summer of 1776, a year after the fighting began, the Second Continental Congress, which had been formed to coordinate the colonial war effort, drew up the colonies' formal Declaration of Independence from Great Britain.

The document was written in large part by Virginian Thomas Jefferson (1743–1826). Completed on July 4, 1776, the Declaration of Independence includes a list of American complaints against the government of King George III. In part, the document reads:

> **The history of the present King of Great Britain is a history of repeated injuries and usurpations [overthrows of power] ... He has kept among us, in times of peace, Standing Armies without the consent of our legislature ... [and given his approval to Parliament's] acts of pretended legislation: For quartering large bodies of armed troops among us: For protecting them, by a mock Trial, from Punishment for any Murders which they should commit on the inhabitants of these States.**

This passage highlights the fact that the quartering of troops was a key issue in the colonies' call for independence. The reference to "Murders which they should commit" also shows that the Boston Massacre still burned in America's memory.

Resentment runs deep

Resentment of quartering was apparent in the colonies. When American forces found it necessary to quarter their own troops during the war with Great Britain, even those who supported the revolution complained. In a letter to Elbridge Gerry (1744–1814)—a Massachusetts representative to the Continental Congress who later served as vice president of the United States—a citizen wrote that such quartering "without the direction of the legislature of the colony . . . is downright and intolerably wrong."

Quartering and the Constitution

Though the Americans did not officially win their independence until 1783, the last major battle was fought and won by the colonists in 1781. The same year, the thirteen former colonies, now states, bound themselves together loosely under the provisions of the Articles of Confederation. But the Articles allowed the states to keep most governmental powers making the new central government very weak.

**Third
Amendment**

A REVOLUTIONARY TRAINING GROUND

Despite the fact that British troops and colonial militias fought side by side throughout the French and Indian War (1754–63), the conflict strained relations between Great Britain and the colonies. The quartering of British soldiers in American homes and the levying of taxes and duties in the colonies to pay for the war angered colonists. After fighting to free the land west of the colonies from the French, Americans were upset when the British Proclamation of 1763 prohibited the colonists from settling in the newly won territory.

In addition to sparking American hostility toward the British government, the French and Indian War provided the colonists with invaluable military experience—experience the Americans would put to use as they took up arms against the seemingly invincible British Army in the American Revolutionary War (1775-83). Even George Washington (1732-99), commander-in-chief of the Continental Army during the Revolutionary War and the first president of the United States, began his military career fighting with the British on the frontiers of the French and Indian War.

In May of 1754, the twenty-two year old Washington was sent by the governor of Virginia to attack Fort Duquesne, a French fort erected where the city of Pittsburgh now stands. Badly outnumbered, Washington's troops retreated to a stone barricade (dubbed Fort Necessity) before eventually surrendering to the French.

Despite this, the state legislatures felt it necessary to guard against future quartering of troops by a central government. Delaware had drafted the *Declaration of Rights and Fundamental Rules* on September 11, 1776, as part of its state constitution. That document included the following stipulation: "That no Soldier ought to be quartered in any House in Time of Peace without the Consent of the Owner; and in Time of War in such Manner only as the Legislature shall direct." The language of this document closely resembles the Third Amendment.

By the time the Articles of Confederation were in place, Maryland, Massachusetts, and New Hampshire had incorporated similar language into their state constitutions (see Introduction).

Washington's defeat at the hands of Great Britain's long-time enemy embarrassed the British government and plans were made for another attack on the French fort. In the summer of 1755, two thousand British troops under General Edward Braddock set out to take Fort Duquesne.

Unfortunately, the enormous army moved very slowly. Washington, serving as an advisor to Braddock, worried that the army's slow progress would give the French time to bring in reinforcements. Washington and others also warned the general that moving his troops in large groups of ordered formations would make them an easy target for the French.

Braddock ignored the warnings, and continued to advance the large European-style formations through the wilderness. Unfortunately, Washington's fears were justified. Hundreds of Native American reinforcements had joined the French troops at Fort Duquesne and were awaiting Braddock's approach. As the general's army made its way through the rough trails and wooded hills near Fort Duquesne, French and Native American soldiers attacked from all sides, firing on the Redcoats from behind trees, rocks and hills. In what became known as the Battle of the Wilderness the attackers utterly destroyed the larger British force.

Washington served in the military until 1759, when he resigned his post as commander-in-chief of the Virginia militia and retired to civilian life. Sixteen years later the seasoned veteran of the French and Indian War returned to battle, leading the Continental Army to victory over the British government he once served.

Making the government stronger—but not too strong

By 1787 many people in the new country felt the need for a stronger central government, especially if the new states were going to interact with other countries from a position of strength. During the summer, delegates from twelve of the thirteen states gathered to discuss the creation of a new government. This Constitutional Convention resulted in the drafting of the United States Constitution (see Introduction).

Adopted in 1788, the new Constitutional government of the United States was established in 1789. Many people, however, felt that the Constitution—which lacked a bill of rights—gave the new government too much power. They worried that without such a bill of rights, the

**Third
Amendment**

*General George
Washington, who
had led his
American troops to
victory over the
British, was a part
of the drafting of
the Constitution,
and the first leader
of the country it
defined.* Courtesy of the
Library of Congress.

people were in danger of losing the very liberties they had fought so hard to win.

One of the concerns was that the constitution gave the new Congress (the legislative branch of the U.S. government) the power to raise a national army but did not restrict the practice of quartering troops in private homes. Virginian Patrick Henry (1736–1799), one of the strongest voices in support of adding a bill of rights to the Constitution, noted in 1788 that

> **One of our first complaints, under the former [British] government, was the quartering of troops upon us. This was one of the principal reasons for dissolving the connection with Great Britain. [Under the new Constitution,] we may have troops in time of peace. They may be billeted in any manner—to tyrannize, oppress, and crush us.**

Henry's statement stressed how important the issue of quartering troops (also known as billeting) had been to the fight for independence and how important it remained.

Concerns over quartering and other issues led the states to almost immediately begin drafting amendments to the Constitution. These early amendments eventually became America's Bill of Rights (see Introduction). Of the eight states that proposed initial amendments to the Constitution, five of them specifically called for a prohibition on the quartering of troops in people's homes.

Third Amendment passes without a fight

James Madison (1751–1836), a Virginian who became the fourth president of the United States, wrote the proposal for a quartering amendment and submitted it to Congress on September 25, 1789. There was such general agreement among Americans against quartering that Madison's proposal passed with little debate.

Some representatives did argue that the amendment should be even stronger. One suggestion was that the amendment simply say "No soldier shall be quartered in any house without the consent of the owner." A majority of representatives voted against this alteration, however, because it did not make any allowances for wartime emergencies.

Passing through Congress unaltered, the amendment was ratified by the three-fourths of the states required by the Constitution on December 15, 1791, when Virginia became the eleventh of the fourteen states then in existence to ratify the amendment.

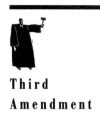

**Third
Amendment**

The Third Amendment Goes to Trial

Since becoming part of the Constitution, the Third Amendment has not been at the center of many debates. In 1965 Supreme Court Justice William O. Douglas included the Third Amendment as part of a constitutional right to privacy in the opinion he wrote for the Court in the case of *Griswold v. Connecticut*. There is, however, no Supreme Court case that specifically involves the Third Amendment protection against quartering soldiers in peacetime.

Landlords and tenants in the lower courts

The Third Amendment has been highlighted in several lower federal court cases. Some legal experts consider the connection to the Third Amendment in these cases weak, but it is interesting to look at a couple of cases to see how different parties have interpreted the amendment.

BEYOND THE BILLETING ISSUE. In *United States v. Valenzuela,* a 1951 case in the California district court, Gus P. Valenzuela argued that the Third Amendment should protect him against being prosecuted by the government for violations of the Housing and Rent Control Act of 1947. Valenzuela argued that the Third Amendment prohibited any government interference with one's home, including matters of rent collection.

The court dismissed the Third Amendment connection, but opponents of government authority have used Valenzuela's interpretation to argue that the Third Amendment prohibits any government intrusion into private lives.

RENTERS PROTECTION, TOO? A more straightforward interpretation of the Third Amendment was put forth by the U.S. Court of Appeals of the Second Circuit in the 1982 case of *Engblom v. Carey.*

Marianne Engblom and Charles Palmer were prison guards at the New York State Mid-Orange Correctional Facility in 1979 who lived in rented quarters on the grounds of the prison facility. When the prison guards went on strike in 1979, National Guard troops were sent to maintain order at the prison.

Engblom and Palmer were given notice and subsequently evicted from their quarters to make room for the National Guard troops. They then filed suit in court claiming that the soldiers had been quartered in their home without their consent. This argument interprets the words "in any house" to mean any building, regardless of whether it is the person's primary home or whether the occupants are renters or owners.

The displaced guards lost their case, however, on various grounds, and there have been no other significant Third Amendment court rulings since.

Quiet Child of the Revolutionary War

The Third Amendment has simply not played a major role in the courts or in the daily live of Americans since the Revolutionary War. This is in

Today, American soldiers are housed in barracks all over the United States and the world.

Reproduced by permission of AP/Wide World Photos.

**Third
Amendment**

large part because there have not been any large-scale incidents of forced peacetime quartering in the United States.

Supreme Court Justice Joseph Story (1779–1845), writing his 1833 *Commentaries on the Constitution,* summed up the issue well. Story wrote:

> **This provision speaks for itself. Its plain object is to secure the perfect enjoyment of that great right of the common law, that a man's house shall be his own castle, privileged against all civil and military intrusions.**

If the Third Amendment has only rarely been invoked since its adoption, its placement in the Bill of Rights nonetheless serves as a reminder of the Revolutionary generation's strong belief that citizens should never be at the mercy of the military in times of peace or war. The amendment's speedy adoption—after almost no debate—emphasizes just how thoroughly this ideal was embraced by an American public that had only recently won its independence from a great military power.

For More Information

Books

Hull, Mary E. *The Boston Tea Party in American History.* Springfield, NJ: Enslow Publishers, Inc., 1999.

Minks, Benton, and Louise Minks. *The French and Indian War.* San Diego, CA: Lucent Books, 1995.

Zall, P. M. *Becoming American: Young People in the American Revolution.* Hamden, CT: Linnet Books, 1993.

Web Sites

American History Online. *Prelude to Revolution: The Boston Massacre.* [Online] http://longman.awl.com/history/ (accessed on January 25, 2001).

Crispus Attucks the Patriot. [Online] http://www.crispusattucks.org/ crispusattucksthepatriot.htm (accessed on January 25, 2001).

The U.S. Constitution Online. [Online] http://www.usconstitution.net (accessed on January 25, 2001).

Sources

Books

Bailyn, Bernard, ed. *Debate on the Constitution: Federalist and Antifederalist Speeches, Articles, and Letters During the Struggle over Ratification.* New York: The Library of America, 1993.

Cushing, Harry Alonso, ed. *The Writings of Samuel Adams, Volume I (1764–1769).* New York: G. P. Putnam's Sons, 1904.

Encyclopedia of World Biography. Detroit: Gale, 1998.

Franklin, Benjamin. *Autobiography and Other Writings: Benjamin Franklin.* Edited by Kenneth Silverman. New York: Penguin USA, 1986.

Holmes, Burnham. *The American Heritage History of the Bill of Rights, Volume 3, The Third Amendment.* Englewood Cliffs, NJ: Silver Burdett Press, 1990.

Madison, James. *Notes of Debates in the Federal Convention of 1787.* New York: W. W. Norton, 1987.

Articles

Bell, Tom W. "The Third Amendment: Forgotten but Not Gone." *William & Mary Bill of Rights Journal.* 2 (1993): 117–50.

Fourth Amendment

The right of the people to be secure in their persons, houses, papers, and effects, against unreasonable searches and seizures, shall not be violated, and no Warrants shall issue, but upon probable cause, supported by Oath or affirmation, and particularly describing the place to be searched, and the persons or things to be seized.

Wiretaps, drug-sniffing dogs, random locker searches, drug raids: These are just some of the tools police and other authorities use to gather evidence of wrongdoing and fight crime in the United States. The Fourth Amendment seeks to balance society's need for effective law enforcement with the individual's rights to privacy and property by prohibiting police from "unreasonably" conducting searches or seizing property as evidence.

Probable Cause and the Particularity Requirement

Before conducting a legal search, a police officer must usually obtain a warrant from a judge or other employee of the court. A warrant is a court document that gives an officer certain limited powers to search for evidence or make arrests.

According to the Fourth Amendment, there are two main conditions that must be met for a warrant to be legal. First, an officer must convince a judge that there is a good reason to issue a warrant. This is called showing probable cause. Second, the warrant must be very specific. This is called the particularity requirement.

An officer shows probable cause by presenting information that would convince a "reasonable person" that a crime has been committed

RATIFICATION FACTS

PROPOSED: Submitted by Congress to the states on September 25, 1789, along with the other nine amendments that comprise the Bill of Rights.

RATIFICATION: Ratified by the required three-fourths of states (eleven of fourteen) on December 15, 1791. Declared to be part of the Constitution on December 15, 1791.

RATIFYING STATES: New Jersey, November 20, 1789; Maryland, December 19, 1789; North Carolina, December 22, 1789; South Carolina, January 19, 1790; New Hampshire, January 25, 1790; Delaware, January 28, 1790; New York, February 24, 1790; Pennsylvania, March 10, 1790; Rhode Island, June 7, 1790; Vermont, November 3, 1791; Virginia, December 15, 1791 (amendment adopted).

and that the person to be searched is probably connected to the crime. To meet the particularity requirement, a warrant must list exactly who and what is to be searched and what type of evidence the officer hopes to find.

Though it establishes some specific conditions for legal searches and the collection of evidence, the wording of the Fourth Amendment leaves plenty of room for interpretation. Some of the questions that have arisen around enforcement of the Fourth Amendment include:

- What is an "unreasonable" search?
- What constitutes probable cause?
- Can an officer seize evidence not listed on a warrant?
- Do all searches require a warrant?
- Can evidence obtained during an unconstitutional search be used in court?
- Are students protected by the Fourth Amendment at school?

These are not questions with simple answers. The Supreme Court has heard hundreds of cases involving such Fourth Amendment issues and used various interpretations of the amendment to establish specific rules concerning police searches and the seizure of property.

Fourth Amendment

Protecting the "Comforts of Society"

In the early 1300s, Britain's king began granting his officials general warrants, which they could use to search any home they wished, seize any property they saw fit, and arrest anyone based on what they found. These warrants, once issued, lasted until the death of the king or queen who issued them. Often these warrants were used to harass people who practiced unpopular religions or who disagreed with the government's policies.

In 1762 the government of King George III (1738–1820) used general warrants to break into the homes and offices of authors, printers, and publishers suspected of being critical of the king. The agents ransacked the suspects' possessions and seized their papers. The victims of the raids sued the government for illegal trespass, but officials argued that they had legal warrants for the searches.

Two of the cases, *Wilkes v. Wood* (1763) and *Entick v. Carrington* (1765), were heard by the same judge, Lord Camden. Camden ruled that the warrants in the cases were not based on facts that justified the searches. In other words, they lacked probable cause.

The practice of using drug-sniffing dogs in airports and at border crossings has become very common in the fight against drug-trafficking.

Reproduced by permission of AP/Wide World Photos.

He also ruled that the warrants were not specific enough, because they ordered the seizure of all of the suspects' papers, rather than those that might have been part of a crime. Such broad warrants, Camden wrote, undermined "all the comforts of society." As a result of Camden's ruling, the men who had been wrongly searched or imprisoned were allowed to sue the government.

Writs of Assistance in America

In Britain's American colonies, customs officials and tax collectors had used general warrants, known as writs of assistance, to conduct random searches since the late seventeenth century. With warrant in hand, British officials could turn entire neighborhoods upside down, seize any property, and arrest anyone based only on their suspicions. In other words, agents in the colonies, like their counterparts in England, had never been required to show probable cause or to specify what they were searching for.

Because warrants were good only during the lifetime of the king who issued them, when King George II (1683–1760) died, all writs given

Today, the Fourth Amendment enables police officers to forcibly enter the hiding places of dangerous criminals with the permission of the courts.

Reproduced by permission of AP/Wide World Photos.

out under his authority became void. Government officials wishing to conduct searches in the colonies had to obtain new warrants under the authority of the new king, George III.

In 1761 merchants in Boston, Massachusetts, went to court to stop new warrants from being granted (*Paxton's Case*). The merchants' attorney, James Otis Jr. (1725–1783), denounced the writs as "the worst instrument of arbitrary power ... that ever was found in our English law book" because they placed "the liberty of every man in the hands of every petty officer."

Otis argued for a fairer process of issuing warrants in which officers would be given the right "to search certain houses" for particular evidence. Warrants, he argued, should only be granted after the official swore under oath "that he suspects such goods to be concealed in those very places he desires to search."

The merchants lost the case, and British officials continued to use general warrants to conduct random searches in the colonies. But Otis's fiery arguments against excessive government intrusion fanned the flames of America's growing revolutionary spirit. After the trial, angry crowds often interfered with customs and revenue agents attempting to enforce general warrants, while some local magistrates (judges) declined to give out the writs of assistance.

Establishing the People's Rights

Growing tension between Great Britain and the American colonies led to the American Revolutionary War (1775–83), in which the colonies separated from the British Empire. The newly independent colonies (now states) formed a loose alliance with each other under the Articles of Confederation in 1781. But in 1788, the states adopted the U.S. Constitution (see chapter one), which established a much stronger central government.

But because nothing in the new Constitution spelled out the people's rights, many worried that the new government might take the very liberties the colonists had fought Great Britain to win. In response to this concern, a number of amendments (additions) defining different rights were proposed to the Constitution. The first ten amendments to be agreed upon by the states are known as the Bill of Rights (see chapter one).

James Madison (1751–1836), a Virginia lawyer who later became the fourth president of the United States, wrote the Fourth Amendment, using Otis's ideas from *Paxton's Case* and from Camden's ruling in *Entick v. Carrington*. With the memory of abusive British searches still fresh in the people's minds, the amendment was officially ratified by the states on December 15, 1791.

Interpreting the Fourth Amendment

The Supreme Court, as established by the Constitution (see chapter one), is the highest court in the United States. Congress (the lawmaking branch of the United States government) decides how many judges sit on the court. The Court originally consisted of six justices (judges), but has included nine justices since 1869. A justice may write an opinion supporting either side of a given case, but the Court's final ruling is left to a simple vote of all the justices.

The justices typically hear appeals of cases first heard by lower courts. (An appeal is a legal request to reconsider a court's ruling.) The Supreme Court is the final interpreter of all federal laws, including the constitutional amendments. The Fourth Amendment, which has played

As times change, the tools that police officers use to enforce the law change as well. Helicopters are now commonly used to search for fleeing suspects, or search for stolen or illegal goods. Reproduced by permission of AP/Wide World Photos.

Fourth Amendment

an important and changing role in criminal justice, provides an excellent illustration of how the Supreme Court's interpretation of a law affects the way in which the law is understood and enforced by the government.

What Warrants a Good Warrant?

Law enforcement officers usually must have a warrant in order to perform a search or seize evidence. But having a warrant isn't always enough. For a warrant to be legal, an officer must show probable cause and meet the particularity requirement by listing exactly what and who are to be searched, and what evidence the officer expects to find.

Showing probable cause

In 1806, the Supreme Court heard its first Fourth Amendment case. The case involved John A. Burford, a Virginia merchant whose temper and behavior were so bad that his neighbors complained to several justices of the peace that they were worried he might commit a crime. In light of their testimony, a court order was issued requiring Burford to pay a bond of $4,000, which he would lose if he committed a crime.

When Burford could not pay the bond (a small fortune at the time) he was arrested and put in jail. When the Supreme Court heard the case, it ordered Burford released from jail. Chief Justice John Marshall (1755–1835) stated that the warrant used to arrest Burford did not comply with any of the Fourth Amendment's requirements. In particular, he stated that the warrant lacked probable cause to suspect a crime had been committed, because it was based solely on testimony that Burford *might* commit a crime.

Five years later, in *Locke v. United States* the Court clearly defined probable cause as "a reasonable ground for belief of guilt" regarding a crime. Without such ground for belief, the court ruled, a warrant was not valid.

Stool pigeons and the Aguilar test

Police often use informants in their work. An informant is someone who offers information to the police. Prior to 1964, an officer could obtain a warrant using only an informant's tip. If an informant told the police a house was used to hide stolen goods, for instance, a police officer could use the tip to get a search warrant.

But in *Aguilar v. Texas* (1964), the Court said an officer must show that an informant is trustworthy and must also explain how the informant came to his or her conclusions. For instance, did the informant witness any wrongdoing or only hear about it secondhand? The judge could then decide whether the informant's tip justified issuing a warrant.

The Supreme Court changed its mind again in *Illinois v. Gates* (1983). There the Court stated that a judge should weigh all evidence when considering a warrant, including tips that fail the *Aguilar* test. This ruling has made it easier for police to obtain warrants using informant tips.

The "Who, What, Where, and When"

To prevent the kind of general searches common in the colonial era, the Fourth Amendment requires warrants to "particularly describe" the areas to be searched and the type of evidence to be seized. Searches that go beyond the specific scope of a warrant are usually not allowed.

Warrants must also name the people to be searched or arrested, and police are generally not allowed to search people not named on a warrant. In *Ybarra v. Illinois* (1979), for instance, the Supreme Court ruled that police could not search a patron in a bar who was not named in their warrant. Officers must also use a warrant within a reasonable period of time after it is issued to meet the particularity requirement.

Shotgun in a shoebox

There are exceptions to the particularity requirement. One of the more common is the plain view rule, which allows officers to seize certain evidence without a warrant if they can see it. For example, an officer with a warrant to search Jim at his house for drugs would normally not be allowed to search Jim's visiting grandmother unless she were also named in the warrant. However, if Jim's grandmother were holding drugs in plain sight during the search, the police could seize the evidence without a warrant.

The plain view rule also applies to evidence that may not be out in the open. If police with a warrant to search for drugs at Jim's house found a stolen shotgun hidden under his bed, the officers could seize the gun without a new warrant, because it was reasonable for them to look for drugs under the bed. On the other hand, if police had a warrant to search for a shotgun and uncovered stolen gems hidden in a shoebox, they could not use the gems as evidence, because there was no reason to search the shoebox for a shotgun.

OFFICER IN JEOPARDY. The court has also ruled that officers may search people for weapons, even if they are not named in a warrant, when the safety of officers or other people in the area may be jeopardized. If officers have a warrant to arrest a particular gang member, for instance, they may search other gang members in the area for weapons while making the arrest.

Are Search Warrants Always Necessary?

The Fourth Amendment establishes requirements for obtaining legal warrants and prohibits unreasonable searches. Nowhere, however, does the amendment say that all searches must begin with a warrant. The "plain view rule" and limited weapon searches allow officers to go beyond the scope of a warrant in certain situations. But officers may also conduct certain kinds of searches with no warrant at all. The Supreme Court has dealt repeatedly with the issue of when and if a search requires a warrant.

Extending the bounds of the Fourth Amendment

In the 1877 case of *Ex Parte Jackson,* postal inspectors argued that the mail was subject to warrantless searches. But the Supreme Court ruled that one's mail is protected against unreasonable search and seizure, just like private papers in one's home. As long as a person's mail is held by the post office, it can only be opened by an official who has obtained a legal warrant. Otherwise, it must remain sealed and secure from prying eyes.

THE CASE OF THE "SEARCHLESS" SEARCH. In *Boyd v. New York* (1886), the import company E. A. Boyd & Sons, was accused of not paying duties (government import fees) on a quantity of imported plate glass. An 1874 federal law gave the government the power to force Boyd & Sons to produce an invoice (receipt) for the glass it had imported. Using the invoice as evidence, the government proved that the company had not paid the duty.

The company protested that the law violated the Fourth Amendment and the Fifth Amendment, which protects defendants from being forced to incriminate themselves (see chapter six). The government argued that the Fourth Amendment applied only to physical searches of private property, and because no such search had been made, no violation had occurred.

The Supreme Court disagreed. Justice Joseph P. Bradley (1813–1892) observed that by forcing defendants to hand over the same type of evidence that might be found in an actual search and seizure without obtaining a warrant, the law violated the Fourth Amendment. Because the law that helped convict Boyd & Sons was deemed unconstitutional, the Court threw out the conviction, despite the fact that evidence showed the company had broken the law.

REASONABLE EXPECTATION OF PRIVACY. In 1967, the Supreme Court established a broad rule of thumb for determining when a search requires a warrant. Federal agents had used electronic listening devices (without a warrant) to eavesdrop on Charles Katz as he talked in a public phone booth. The police later used recordings of these calls to prove Katz was involved in illegal gambling activities.

The Supreme Court, however, found that the government eavesdropping met the definition of a search and seizure under the Fourth Amendment, because the actions "violated the privacy upon which [Katz] justifiably relied while using the telephone booth." The case established that if a defendant has a "reasonable expectation of privacy" when a search is performed, a warrant is required.

Fourth Amendment

Officers are allowed to search a person's car if they suspect that the driver might be carrying something illegal.

Reproduced by permission of AP/Wide World Photos.

**Fourth
Amendment**

*Police officers are
able to stop and
frisk a person who is
suspected of being
guilty of a crime.*

Search and seizure without a warrant

Although the reasonable expectation of privacy standard was used to expand Katz's protection from searches outside his home, the same rule of thumb has since been used to justify a variety of warrantless searches.

ON WHEELS. As early 1925 (*Carrol v. United States*) the Court allowed warrantless searches of automobiles if the officer had probable cause to believe the vehicle contained illegal goods, because a vehicle might slip away before an officer could obtain a warrant. But in *Cardwell v. Lewis* (1974), the Court used the *Katz* standard to further justify vehicle searches stating that "One has a lesser expectation of privacy in a motor vehicle because its function is transportation and it seldom serves as one's residence."

Though this ruling allows for many vehicle searches, the Supreme Court has stated that full vehicle searches are not allowed when a driver is stopped for a traffic violation and the officer has no probable cause to suspect other criminal conduct (*Knowles v. Iowa* [1998]).

THE GREAT OUTDOORS. The expectation of privacy standard has also been used to allow searches of open fields without a warrant, except in the area "immediately around the home." However, even there, the Court has ruled that a person does not have a reasonable expectation of privacy from aerial surveillance. In light of these rulings, searches conducted by police helicopters or airplanes rarely require a warrant, and aerial searches of private property for marijuana fields and other contraband have become routine.

THE STOP AND FRISK. The case of *Terry v. Ohio* (1968) created another form of warrantless search. Prior to this case, police needed to have probable cause before making an arrest. But in *Terry,* the Court ruled that a police officer need only reach two conclusions to justify a warrantless stop and frisk: first, that criminal activity may be going on, and second, that the suspect may be armed and dangerous.

In such cases, police can conduct a "carefully limited search" of the suspect's outer clothing for weapons for the safety of officers and others in the area. Some people argue that the decision to allow "suspicion-based" searches without a warrant considerably weakens the probable cause requirement for searches.

An officer in "hot pursuit" of a suspected felon (someone who has just committed a crime) may conduct a warrantless search for the fleeing suspect. And in cases where evidence may readily disappear, as in blood samples from drunken drivers, an officer may seize that evidence without a warrant.

What to Do with "Bad" Evidence

Despite such exceptions, most searches do require a warrant, and most warrants must meet the particularity requirement and show probable cause. But what happens to evidence when the police break these rules? The Fourth Amendment is silent on the subject, leaving it to the Supreme Court to decide just what can be done with the evidence of unconstitutional searches. Those rulings have not always been consistent.

Why waste evidence?

In *Boyd v. United States* (see above) the Supreme Court leaned toward excluding illegally obtained evidence. But in *Adams v. New York* (1904) the Court ruled that evidence seized by the government that was not listed on a search warrant could be used against the defendants. The Court

**Fourth
Amendment**

stated that English courts and nearly all U.S. courts had historically refused to throw out evidence just because it was obtained illegally. The Court reasoned that a criminal should not go free because the police made a mistake.

The exclusionary rule is born

In the case of *Weeks v. United States* (1914), the Supreme Court changed its mind. Officers had searched the home of Frederick Weeks without a warrant and seized envelopes that linked Weeks to illegal gambling activities.

Weeks claimed that the search and seizure violated his Fourth and Fifth Amendment rights and that his personal property should be returned to him. The government lawyers assumed that the *Adams v. New York* decision allowed them to use the evidence regardless of how it was obtained.

But the Supreme Court agreed that Weeks' property (which just happened to be the evidence against him) should have been returned to him because it had been seized illegally. And, the Court reasoned, if his property was returned, it could not be used to convict him.

These harmless looking plants being seized from someone's property are actually marijuana plants and are illegal to grow. Reproduced by permission of AP/Wide World Photos.

"If letters and private documents can (be seized illegally) and held and used in evidence," wrote Justice William Rufus Day (1849–1923), "the protection of the Fourth Amendment] might as well be stricken from the Constitution." The idea that illegally obtained evidence should not be used against a defendant, even when it proves the defendant's guilt, became known as the exclusionary rule and stands as one of the Court's most important and controversial interpretations of law to date.

Excluding fruits of a poisonous tree

Other cases have expanded the scope of the exclusionary rule. In *Silverthorne Lumber Co. v. United States* (1920), police officers made copies of illegally seized books and papers before returning the evidence to the defendants. The government then used the copies to convict the company of wrongdoing. The government attorneys argued that the Fourth Amendment only required the return of illegally seized evidence.

But the Supreme Court disagreed. Justice Oliver Wendell Holmes (1841–1935) argued that evidence gained in violation of the Fourth Amendment should not be used in any way. This assertion that any evidence obtained as result of illegally obtained evidence should not be used is know as excluding the "fruit of the poisonous tree."

Hot evidence on a silver platter

In seeming contradiction to this ruling was the so-called silver platter doctrine. The limits of government found in the Bill of Rights initially only applied to the federal government, not the individual state governments. The Supreme Court began to extend the reach of the Bill of Rights to include state government in the 1920s (for more information, see chapter fourteen) but the process took several decades to complete. Therefore, until the 1960s, different rules applied at the state and federal levels. This could lead to complicated situations when local and federal law enforcement agencies cooperated on a case.

In *Byars v. United States* (1927) the Supreme Court ruled that federal officials could use evidence that had been seized illegally by state police as long as state officers had not conducted the search on behalf of the federal government, and no federal officers participated in the search. In other words, as long as the state government served the evidence up on "a silver platter" to the federal officials, the evidence could be used. In *Elkins v. United States* (1960), the Court did away with the silver platter doctrine, and a year later the states were also prohibited also prohibited from using illegally obtained evidence.

WEIGHING SOCIETY'S INTERESTS

The Supreme Court has established particular situations where a warrantless search may be legal, such as when evidence is in plain view or when an officer is in hot pursuit of a felon. But the Court has also determined that there are certain people and places where society's interests outweigh an individual's Fourth Amendment rights.

Railroad employees and customs officers, for instance, can be searched and tested for drugs without a warrant because their jobs involve public safety. Along America's borders, customs officials have the power to search anyone without a warrant, probable cause, or suspicion because the nation has an interest in protecting its boundaries. Prisons are another place where people have no Fourth Amendment protections.

Many lower courts have ruled that locker searches, drug-sniffing dogs, and the search of student vehicles on school property are legal and that school officials may conduct such searches without warrants or probable cause.

The Supreme Court, however, has heard very few cases on the subject of searches on public school grounds. In a 1985 decision, the Court recognized that although public school students enjoy certain Fourth Amendment protections, neither probable cause nor the warrant requirement is necessary because school officials are government

Making States Play by the Rules

The Supreme Court initially implemented the Fourth Amendment in the states without compelling the local governments to abide by the exclusionary rule. In the case of *Wolf v. Colorado* (1949) a local sheriff entered the office of Dr. Julius Wolf with a warrant and seized documents that were later used to convict Wolf of performing illegal abortions. Wolf appealed to the Supreme Court, and the Court ruled that the Fourth Amendment did apply to the states (see chapter fourteen).

However, the Court ruled that the states did not have to exclude illegally obtained evidence, and Wolf's conviction was not overturned.

agents when they carry out searches. As a result, they may conduct a search based on their reasonable suspicions.

One concept the courts have pointed to in making these rulings is that school officials behave *in locus parentis*—in the place of parents. In other words, while students are at school, teachers and administrators have the same rights and responsibilities as a child's parent. Other courts have pointed to the fact that lockers, desks and other property that belongs to the schools never becomes the property of the students, and therefore is never protected from a school search. However, the Supreme Court has never specifically ruled on this issue.

In *Vernonia School District v. Acton,* the Court did rule that random drug tests of student athletes were legal. In the opinion, the Court stated that students could choose avoid the searches by choosing not to play sports. The Court also used the expectation of privacy standard, saying that student athletes had a decreased expectation of privacy because they played sports.

One area where both the Supreme Court and the lower courts have seemed to draw the line is strip searches of students. Both Courts have ruled that even partial bodily searches of students were an invasion of privacy. In a Circuit Court of Appeals case involving the routine use of drug-sniffing dogs and strip searches in schools, the Court stated that a strip search of a young girl was an "invasion of constitutional rights of some magnitude."

The Court stated that the exclusionary rule was only one way to deter illegal searches, and states were free to choose others, such as allowing citizens to sue officials who performed illegal searches. Disagreeing with the ruling. Justice Frank Murphy (1890–1949) wrote, "The conclusion is inescapable that but one remedy exists to deter violations of the search and seizure clause." Namely, the exclusionary rule.

Applying the rules

Because most criminal cases in the United States are tried at the state level, where the exclusionary rule was not enforced, the rule had very little effect on criminal law through much of the twentieth century.

Fourth Amendment

This changed with the 1961 case of *Mapp v. Ohio.* After being tipped off that Dollree Mapp might be in possession of bomb-making materials, police officers (claiming to have a warrant) broke into Mapp's home and ransacked her possessions. The officers claimed to have found obscene materials during their search, and Mapp was later convicted of violating a state obscenity law based on this evidence. However, no warrant was ever produced at the trial.

When the Supreme Court heard the case, the state of Ohio pointed to the decision in *Wolf,* arguing that even if the search had been made without a warrant, nothing prevented the state from using the illegally obtained evidence. The Court, however took this opportunity to overturn the *Wolf* ruling and extended the exclusionary rule to the states.

Few developments in constitutional law have changed the landscape of law enforcement so much or have been as controversial. Opponents denied that there was any constitutional basis for the rule and argued that it punished officers for making mistakes while letting criminals go free.

Proponents of the exclusionary rule believed it was the only way to give the Fourth Amendment teeth and prevent abuses of police power. Justice Tom Clark (1899–1977) wrote, "[W]e can no longer permit [the Fourth Amendment] to be revocable at the whim of any police officer." He argued that although the exclusionary rule allowed some criminals to go free, the tradeoff was worthwhile because "nothing can destroy a government more quickly than its failure to observe its own laws."

Allowing for Honest Mistakes

In the 1984 case of *United States v. Leon,* the Court staked out a bit of middle ground between the opposing views of the exclusionary rule. A magistrate had issued a defective search warrant in a drug case, and because of the mistake, drug evidence seized in a raid was excluded from a lower court trial. However, the Supreme Court reversed that decision, ruling that evidence obtained under a warrant that is later ruled to be invalid could be used if the law enforcement officer acted reasonably.

In other words, the Court said that criminals should not benefit from honest mistakes. Justice Byron R. White (1917–) wrote that the exclusionary rule was created "to deter police misconduct rather than to punish the errors of judges and magistrates."

The Court broadened the so-called good faith exception in *Arizona v. Evans* (1995). A court employee had mistakenly listed Isaac Evans as the subject of a misdemeanor arrest warrant. A police officer who stopped Evans for a traffic violation searched him under the authority of that warrant and found marijuana in his possession. At the trial, Evans succeeded in having the marijuana evidence suppressed.

But the Supreme Court voted to allow the evidence, arguing that evidence seized as a result of a clerical error is admissible at trial, since the exclusionary rule's purpose was to deter *intentional* police abuses.

Critics of the *Evans* and *Leon* rulings, on the other hand, have argued that the good faith exception gives police a free ticket to abuse their search and seizure powers.

The Elastic Shield

The protections provided by the Fourth Amendment, though simply stated, have not proved as simple to interpret. Since first Fourth Amendment case in 1804, the Supreme Court has limited the government's search and seizure power (in cases such as *Weeks, Katz,* and *Mapp*) and expanded it (in cases such as *Adams* and *Terry.*

Regular searches and raids of known areas of drug-trafficking can result in large quantities of drugs being taken off the streets. Reproduced by permission of AP/Wide World Photos.

**Fourth
Amendment**

POLICE, THIEVES, AND THE USE OF THE STOLEN EVIDENCE

The Fourth Amendment applies specifically to the actions of law enforcement officers and court officials. But does it protect against searches by people other than the police? The answer, surprisingly, is usually no. In fact, the Court has ruled that evidence gained by illegal methods is admissible (useable) in court, as long as the police weren't involved in getting it.

In 1918, as America was fighting World War I (a conflict largely between European nations that that lasted from 1914 to 1918) the U.S. Intelligence Department became convinced that Felix Gouled was involved in a conspiracy to defraud the government. The government enlisted the help of an army private who knew Gouled to help gather evidence against him. The soldier visited Gouled at his office on a "social call" and while he was there, he took some of his host's papers and turned them over to the federal agents.

The government used evidence from the stolen papers to show probable cause for a search warrant and used the evidence gathered with the warrant to arrest Gouled and charge him with conspiracy. In

Like other amendments, the Fourth Amendment has been interpreted and reinterpreted, often in response to the changing values and conditions of a given time. Even if its exact dimensions have been stretched and shrunk, the Fourth Amendment still provides Americans with an exceptional shield against intrusive police searches and unjustifiable seizures of private property.

For More Information

Books

Wetterer, Charles M. *The Fourth Amendment: Search and Seizure.* Springfield, NJ: Enslow Publishers, 1998.

Jacobs, Thomas A., J.D. *What Are My Rights? 95 Questions and Answers about Teens and the Law.* Minneapolis, MN: Free Spirit Publishing, 1997.

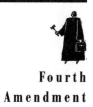
1921, Gouled's case came before the Supreme Court, and the Court ruled that none of the evidence, neither that stolen by the soldier nor any of the evidence found during the later searches, could be used.

At the time the Supreme Court did not allow the seizure of papers that weren't in themselves illegal. In order to be seized, evidence had to be contraband (illegal goods) such as drugs or stolen property. However, the Court also ruled that because a government law enforcement agency had urged the soldier to steal the evidence, the soldier was essentially conducting a government search without a warrant, and therefore the evidence was excluded.

Interstingly, that same year the court heard *Burdeau v. McDowell* (1921). In that case, a man stole evidence without any governmental authority and later turned it over to law enforcement officials. The Supreme Court ruled that because the Fourth Amendment, and therefore the exclusionary rule, only apply to government agents, evidence that is illegally obtained by a person with no connections to law enforcement could be used in court.

In other words, a police officer cannot enter your home and take useable evidence without a warrant, but a burglar probably can.

Dolan, Jr., Edward F. *Protect Your Legal Rights: A Handbook for Teenagers.* New York, Julian Messner, 1983.

Gottfried, Ted. *Privacy: Individual Right v. Social Needs.* Brookfield, CT: Millbrook Press, 1994, 112 pp.

Hoobler, Dorothy & Thomas. *Your Right to Privacy.* New York: Franklin Watts, 1986.

Meltzer, Milton. *The Bill of Rights.* New York: Thomas Y. Crowell, 1990.

Web sites

Cyberspace Law Institute, Social Science Electronic Publishing . *Cyberspace Law Lessons; Privacy and the Fourth Amendment.* [Online] http://www.ssrn.com/update/lsn/cyberspace/lessons/priv04.html (accessed on January 25, 2001).

The Fourth Amendment.[Online] http://www.rowan.edu/business/faculty/
byrd/hrslides/ (accessed on January 25, 2001).

Sources

Books

Hall, Kermit L., ed. *Oxford Companion to The Supreme Court of the
United States.* New York: Oxford University Press, 1992.

Killian, Johnny H., and George A. Costello, eds. *The Constitution of the
United States of America—Analysis and Interpretation—Annotation
of Cases Decided by the Supreme Court of the United States to June
29, 1992.* Prepared by the Congressional Research Service, Library
of Congress, 103d Congress, 1st session, 1993, Doc. 103–06.
Washington, D.C.: U.S. Government Printing Office, 1996.

Articles

Amar, Akhil Reed. "The Fourth Amendment, Boston, and the Writs of
Assistance." *Suffolk University Law Review,* No. 30. 1996: 53.

Bradley, Craig M. "Constitutional Protection for Private Papers."
Harvard Civil Rights-Civil Liberties Law Review. Fall 1981: 461.

Maclin, Tracey. "The Complexity of the Fourth Amendment: A
Historical Review." *Boston University Law Review,* No. 77.
December 1997: 925.

Mickenberg, Ira. "Court Settles on Narrower View of 4th Amendment."
The National Law Journal, No. 17. July 31, 1995: 48.

Norton, Jerry E. "The Exclusionary Rule Reconsidered: Restoring the
Status Quo Ante." *Wake Forest Law Review,* No. 33. Summer
1998: 261.

Schnapper, Eric. "Unreasonable Searches and Seizures of Papers."
Virginia Law Review, No. 71. September 1985: 869.

Shotzberger, Keith. "Overview of the Fourth Amendment." *Georgetown
Law Journal,* No. 85. April 1997: 821.

Stewart, Potter. "The Road to *Mapp v. Ohio* and Beyond: The Origins,
Development and Future of the Exclusionary Rule in Search-And-
Seizure Cases." *Columbia Law Review,* No. 83. October
1983: 1365.

Fifth Amendment

No person shall be held to answer for a capital, or otherwise infamous crime, unless on a presentment or indictment of a Grand Jury, except in cases arising in the land or naval forces, or in the Militia, when in actual service in time of War or public danger; nor shall any person be subject for the same offence to be twice put in jeopardy of life or limb; nor shall be compelled in any criminal case to be a witness against himself, nor be deprived of life, liberty, or property, without due process of law; nor shall private property be taken for public use, without just compensation.

The Fifth Amendment is something of a miniature Bill of Rights itself. At first glance the amendment appears to be concerned with fairly technical legal issues. But in fact, the Fifth Amendment's five separate clauses provide some of the Constitution's broadest and strongest protections against government abuse of power.

The following are short descriptions of each of the Fifth Amendment's five clauses:

- **The Grand Jury Clause:** States that a person accused of a federal crime must be formally charged by a grand jury (an impartial group of citizens) before being brought to trial.

- **The Double Jeopardy Clause:** Prohibits the government from trying a person more than once for the same crime.

- **The Self-incrimination Clause:** Gives individuals the right to remain silent if their words might be used against them in court. Refusing to answer questions for this reason is sometimes called "taking the fifth," in reference to the Fifth Amendment.

Fifth Amendment

RATIFICATION FACTS

PROPOSED: Submitted by Congress to the states on September 25, 1789, along with the other nine amendments that comprise the Bill of Rights.

RATIFICATION: Ratified by the required three-fourths of states (eleven of fourteen) on December 15, 1791. Declared to be part of the Constitution on December 15, 1791.

RATIFYING STATES: New Jersey, November 20, 1789; Maryland, December 19, 1789; North Carolina, December 22, 1789; South Carolina, January 19, 1790; New Hampshire, January 25, 1790; Delaware, January 28, 1790; New York, February 24, 1790; Pennsylvania, March 10, 1790; Rhode Island, June 7, 1790; Vermont, November 3, 1791; Virginia, December 15, 1791 (amendment adopted).

- **The Due Process Clause:** Prohibits the government from taking any legal actions or passing any laws that unfairly deprive a person of life, liberty, or property.

- **The Eminent Domain Clause:** Establishes the government's right to take private property for public use (such as building roads); but it also requires the government to pay a fair price for the property it seizes.

Origins of the Fifth Amendment

Tension between Great Britain and its colonies in America in the middle of the eighteenth century eventually led to the outbreak of the American Revolutionary War in 1775. By 1783 the thirteen American colonies had won their independence from the British Empire. The colonies (now independent states) united under the terms of a document known as the Articles of Confederation.

Under the Articles of Confederation, the individual states (the former colonies) kept most of their governmental power, while the federal (central) government was left quite weak. Within a few years it became apparent that the new nation would require a more powerful central government, especially when dealing with other countries. In 1788 the thirteen original states adopted the United States Constitution (see Introduction), which established a strong national government with power divided among a powerful president, Congress (the legislative or law-making body of government), and the Supreme Court.

The Bill of Rights

Nothing in the new Constitution, however, spelled out the people's rights, and many worried that the new government would become too powerful. To limit the government's power, a number of amendments (corrections) to the Constitution were proposed immediately after it was ratified by the states. The first ten of these amendments are known as Bill of Rights (see Introduction). These amendments sought to outline the people's most basic rights.

The Fifth Amendment was written by James Madison, (1751–1836), a Virginia lawyer who later became the fourth president of the United States. Madison wrote a number of the amendments in the Bill of Rights, which were ratified together in 1791 (see Introduction).

One of the rights guaranteed by the Fifth Amendment is that no one can be forced to testify against himself in court. Lt. Col. Oliver North pleaded the Fifth Amendment when testifying in front of Congress in the Iran-Contra hearings. Reproduced by permission of Archive Photos, Inc.

**Fifth
Amendment**

Something borrowed, something new

Many of the rights and protections listed in the Bill of Rights can be traced to English common law. (Common law refers to the entire English legal tradition.) In fact, English common law granted English citizens most of the rights outlined in the Fifth Amendment. But the British government had not always honored these rights in England or in the American colonies. So when it came time to propose amendments to the Constitution, people hoped to firmly reestablish the rights that were supposedly guaranteed under English common law, including the protections found in the Fifth Amendment.

The Fifth Amendment and the Supreme Court

The rights and protections found in the Fifth Amendment are stated in relatively simple language. But the simple language leaves certain questions unanswered about how each amendment should be applied in particular cases. Under the Constitution, the Supreme Court has the power to interpret the laws of the land, including the Constitution and its amendments.

The Supreme Court is the highest court in the United States. Congress (the law-making branch of the United States government) decides how many judges sit on the court. The Court originally consisted of six justices (judges), but since 1869 it has included nine justices.

Typically, the Supreme Court hears appeals of cases that were first heard by lower courts. An appeal is a legal request to have a higher court reconsider another court's ruling. The Court's decisions in a case are decided by a simple vote of the justices. The Court's decisions can have a huge impact on how a law is understood and enforced. Over the years, a number of Supreme Court cases have helped clear up some of the questions raised by the Fifth Amendment.

The Grand Jury Clause

The Grand Jury Clause states that "No person shall be held to answer for a crime, unless on a bill of indictment of a Grand Jury." (This requirement does not apply to trials within the military.) Like a regular trial jury, a grand jury is made up of citizens called together by the government to settle a legal issue. Unlike a regular jury, a grand jury does not decide whether or not a person is guilty of a crime. Instead, the group (usually sixteen to twenty-three men and women) decide whether there is enough evidence against a person to justify bringing him or her to trial.

Because the courts are part of the government, it is possible for a government to abuse the power to bring citizens to trial. The government could use the courts to harass a person, for example, by repeatedly putting the person on trial for made-up charges. The grand jury is seen as a protection against this sort of government harassment, because the government must prove that it has a good reason to believe the accused person should be put on trial.

Bills of indictment

After a grand jury is called together, the government's lawyer (the prosecutor) prepares a bill of indictment. A bill of indictment is a document that explains the case and lists the evidence that the government has collected against the accused. A grand jury may choose to look at any or all of the evidence listed. The jurors may also question witnesses directly or require them to produce documents as evidence.

If the grand jury finds that the prosecutor has a reasonable amount of evidence to accuse the defendant, it can decide that the bill of indictment is a "true bill" and issue an indictment (a formal charge) against the accused person. However, if the grand jury decides there is simply not enough evidence to link the accused to a particular crime, it can rule that there is "no bill," in which case the person is not charged with a crime.

A buffer between the courts and the people

England had a long tradition of requiring a group of citizens to formally accuse a person of a crime before a trial could begin. This group, known as a grand assize (uh-SEEZ) could identify suspects, present evidence, and determine whether to make an accusation. The grand assize was originally created to give the government greater power, by taking the power to formally accuse someone out of the hands of the church and the nobles (aristocrats). By the end of the seventeenth century, however, these grand juries were viewed as a protection against unfair government prosecutions, because the practice put a group of citizens between the accused and the courts.

In America all the colonies had some type of grand jury system in place by 1683. And in the years leading up to the American Revolution, grand juries (made up of colonists) were often sympathetic to those who resisted British rule. For example, when groups of colonists in Boston

Fifth Amendment

angrily (and sometimes violently) protested the Stamp Act (a new British tax system) in 1765, a grand jury in Boston refused to indict the leaders of the protests.

With such events in mind at the time the Bill of Rights was written, the grand jury was viewed as an important protection against unjustified trials.

What can a grand jury hear?

Because it does not decide whether or not someone is guilty, a grand jury may hear evidence that is normally not admissible at a trial. For example, if a witness testifies about what someone else said they saw, that testimony is called "hearsay." Such second-hand evidence is not allowable in a trial, but it may be presented to a grand jury.

Frank Costello, a noted gangster in the 1940s and 1950s, was convicted of federal income tax evasion in the 1950s. Costello argued that his conviction should be overturned (thrown out) because the grand jury that indicted him had only heard hearsay evidence. In *Costello v. United States* (1956), however, the Supreme Court denied Costello's request, noting that the Fifth Amendment does not say what kind of evidence a grand jury needs to hear in order to indict someone. But even when such evidence is heard by a grand jury, a prosecutor still cannot use hearsay in the actual trial.

Just a rubber stamp?

Some critics have argued that the grand jury is a mere tool of the prosecutor, "rubber stamping" (automatically agreeing with) the prosecutor's wishes. And in fact, the procedures used in a grand jury investigation do seem to be stacked against the accused.

NOT ALLOWED TO STICK UP FOR YOURSELF. A person named in the bill of indictment is not given a chance to present evidence in his or her defense to the grand jury. Nor is the accused allowed to cross-examine the witnesses called during the grand jury's investigation. In *United States v. Wong* (1977), the Court even ruled that witnesses need not be warned that they have the right not to incriminate themselves (see "The Self-incrimination Clause" section).

THE WHOLE TRUTH? The prosecutor does not even have to present evidence that seems to help the accused. In *United States v. Williams* (1992) the Supreme Court examined what, if any, regulations a court can impose on a prosecutor in presenting evidence to a grand jury.

A Tulsa, Oklahoma, investor named John Williams was indicted by a federal grand jury for giving false financial reports to a federally insured bank in order to obtain a loan. While some evidence showed that Williams did fill the reports out incorrectly, the prosecutor also had evidence showing that Williams probably did not know he had done so. Preparing false reports by mistake is a lesser crime than doing it on purpose. The prosecutor, however, did not show this evidence to the grand jury, and Williams was indicted for the greater crime.

Williams wanted the indictment dismissed because the prosecutor had not presented all the evidence. The Supreme Court, however, pointed out that nothing in the Constitution or the Fifth Amendment required a prosecutor to present such favorable evidence to a grand jury.

Critics of the grand jury system note that a grand jury is supposed to act as a shield against unjustified prosecutions, but it is only allowed to hear evidence against the accused.

Defending the grand jury system

Though it appears the deck is stacked against the accused, defenders of the grand jury point out that the system allows citizens to participate in the charging process. Furthermore, it is important to remember that a grand jury's main function is to make sure the prosecutor has a reasonable amount of evidence to begin a trial. And if a person *is* indicted by a grand jury, the accused is given an opportunity to present his or her defense during the actual trial.

Grand juries in the states

The Bill of Rights amendments were originally intended to apply to the actions of the federal government, not to the individual states. Since they were ratified, however, the Supreme Court has ruled that all of the limits on government power also apply to state governments. In fact, all the clauses in the Fifth Amendment have been applied to the states, except the grand jury clause.

One of the reasons the grand jury requirement has not been applied to the states is that the Court has found that states can provide the same protection against unfair trials by using other methods, such as pretrial hearings. In a pretrial hearing, a judge, rather than a grand jury, considers whether the government's evidence justifies an indictment. Nonetheless, many states have some grand jury systems in place. Most states, however, use the grand jury only for cases involving the most serious crimes, such as first-degree murder.

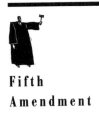

The Double Jeopardy Clause

Like the Grand Jury Clause, the Double Jeopardy Clause is intended to protect citizens from unfair prosecution. The clause prevents the government from repeatedly putting a person on trial for the same crime until the person is convicted. Madison's first draft for the Double Jeopardy Clause stated that "No person shall be subject to more than one punishment or one trial for the same offense." This wording, however, seemed to prevent defendants from appealing their convictions. Under common law (English and American legal tradition), people convicted of crimes have the right to seek such appeals.

To prevent confusion, the clause was changed to state that no person shall be "twice put in jeopardy of life or limb" for the same offense. (To be put in jeopardy is to be put in danger.) The Double Jeopardy Clause thus prohibits the government from putting a person in danger of being punished more than once for the same crime. But it does not stop a person who has been found guilty of a crime (and is therefore still in jeopardy of life and limb) from seeking an appeal.

How does jeopardy double?

The Double Jeopardy Clause seems simple enough. A person found innocent of a crime cannot be put on trial again for the same crime, nor can that person be punished twice for the same crime. Nonetheless, the clause leaves certain technical questions unanswered, leaving it to the Supreme Court to better define the elements of the Double Jeopardy Clause.

When does jeopardy begin?

In *Downum v. United States* (1963) the Supreme Court defined when a person is first considered to be in jeopardy. This can be an important issue when deciding a double jeopardy case, because until a person is put in jeopardy, the protection against double jeopardy is meaningless. In *Downum* the Court ruled that in a trial with a jury (a group of citizens who determine a defendant's guilt or innocence) jeopardy begins as soon as the jury is sworn in. In some criminal trials, however, there is no jury. Instead a judge decides the defendant's guilt or innocence. In these trials jeopardy begins when the first witness is sworn in.

These rules mean that a person can be arrested and indicted by a grand jury without legally being in jeopardy, and as long as the charges are dropped before jeopardy begins, a person can be brought to trial later for the same crime.

When does jeopardy end?

It is also important to know when jeopardy officially ends. In certain situations a trial can end without taking a person out of jeopardy, in which case a second trial merely continues the original jeopardy. Here are some of the ways a trial may end:

- **Acquittal:** If a defendant is acquitted (found not guilty) in a trial, jeopardy ends. The person may not be tried for the crime again even if new evidence is discovered.

- **Dismissal:** A judge may dismiss (throw out) a case at any time during a trial for any number of reasons. The judge may decide, for example, that there is simply not enough evidence to justify a trial. If the case is dismissed after jeopardy has begun, the defendant cannot be tried again. However, if the judge dismisses the case before jeopardy starts (before the first witness or jury member has been sworn in) then the government can bring a defendant to trial again at a later date.

- **Conviction and appeal:** If a person is convicted (found guilty) in a trial, the Double Jeopardy Clause does not prevent the defendant from appealing the conviction. However, the defendant is considered to be under the original jeopardy during the appeal process. If a higher court overturns (throws out) a conviction because there was not enough evidence in the original trial, then jeopardy ends and the defendant cannot be tried again.

However, if the conviction is overturned because a mistake was made during the original trial (such as allowing evidence that was obtained without a search warrant [see chapter four]) then original jeopardy continues. The higher court may then order a second trial in which the mistake is corrected without violating the Fifth Amendment.

When are the same actions not the same offense?

There are several situations in which a person can be brought to trial more than once for the same set of actions without violating the Fifth Amendment.

CIVIL AND CRIMINAL TRIALS. The Fifth Amendment protection against double jeopardy only covers criminal cases. In a criminal case the government seeks to punish a person who has committed a crime. For example, putting a person in prison for assault (attacking someone) punishes the attacker.

**Fifth
Amendment**

*O.J. Simpson was
tried twice for the
suspected murder of
his ex-wife and her
friend—once in
criminal court and
once in civil court.*

Civil trials, on the other hand, are held in order to compensate (pay) a person who has been hurt by someone else's actions. The victim of the above assault, for instance, might bring a civil case against the attacker to cover his hospital costs after the attack.

Because the two kinds of trials serve different purposes, a person may be tried in a civil case and in a criminal case for the same actions, without violating the Fifth Amendment. And because the two trials are entirely separate, it is possible for the cases to have different outcomes.

A famous example of separate civil and criminal outcomes occurred in the mid-1990s, when former professional football star O. J. Simpson was charged with the double murder of his ex-wife and her friend. Based on the evidence at the criminal trial, a jury found Simpson not guilty, preventing the government from ever trying him again for those murders. However, the criminal trial did not prevent the victims' families from bringing a civil complaint against Simpson. In the civil trial a jury decided that Simpson was responsible for the deaths and ordered him to compensate both victims' families for their loss.

DUAL SOVEREIGNTY. The United States has two major layers of sovereignty (government authority): the federal government and the individual state governments. Some criminal actions can break both federal and state laws. In such cases both governments may prosecute a defendant without violating the Double Jeopardy Clause. The Supreme Court announced the so-called dual sovereignty doctrine (principle) in *United States v. Lanza* (1922). In that case the Court ruled that an action that violates the laws of two sovereigns (governments) constitutes a separate offense against each government. Therefore, separate trials are allowed for each crime.

Despite these exceptions, the Double Jeopardy Clause is an effective protection against repeated government prosecutions: in most cases, once a defendant is found innocent of a crime, the government cannot bring that person back to trial for that crime.

The Self-incrimination Clause

The Self-incrimination Clause, which states that no person "shall be compelled in any criminal case to be a witness against himself," is perhaps the most well-known element of the Fifth Amendment. The familiar scene in movies and on television in which police officers inform suspects of their "right to remain silent" is directly related to the legal history of the Fifth Amendment. And when individuals "take the fifth" they are refusing to provide information that might be used against them in a criminal prosecution.

Tortured beginnings

The purpose of the Self-incrimination Clause is to prohibit the government from compelling (forcing) a person to confess to a crime. The right against self-incrimination became part of English law with the trial of John Lilburne in 1637. Lilburne was brought to trial in England for smuggling banned religious booklets into England. During his trial, he refused to take an oath requiring him to answer truthfully any question asked of him. Lilburne claimed the court wanted to trap him and argued that the "law of God and the law of the land" supported his right against self-accusation. Lilburne was whipped and punished in public for refusing to take the oath. But public outcry led Parliament (the British government's law-making body) to declare Lilburne's punishment illegal, and the government eventually recognized a person's right against self-incrimination.

**Fifth
Amendment**

A POLICE BEATING AND DUAL SOVEREIGNTY

In 1991 a group of white police officers in Los Angeles, California, were videotaped beating Rodney G. King, an African American, during an arrest. The officers involved in the assault were brought up on charges, but in April 1992 a jury acquitted them. The verdict touched off a series of riots in Los Angeles that were among the worst in U.S. history.

On the evening of the arrest, King was driving his automobile when a highway police officer attempted to pull him over. King, who had been drinking, fled the scene (he later testified that he was afraid he would be returned to prison for violating his parole). After a high-speed chase involving a number of police vehicles, the police eventually pulled King over. When King got out of his car, four officers—Stacey C. Koon, Laurence M. Powell, Timothy E. Wind, and Theodore J. Briseno—kicked and hit King more than fifty times with their batons while he struggled on the ground.

George Holliday, an amateur photographer who was nearby, videotaped eighty-one seconds of the beating. The videotape was shown on national television and became a symbol of complaints about police brutality. The four officers were charged with assault with a deadly weapon, the use of excessive force, and filing a false police report. During the trial, the prosecution used the videotape as its principal evidence and did not have King testify. The defense also used the videotape to argue that King was resisting arrest and that the violence was necessary to subdue him. But the defense also contended that the videotape distorted the events of that night because it did not capture what happened before and after the eighty-one seconds of tape recording.

Lilburne was a member of the Puritan religious movement, as were many of the original American colonists in Massachusetts. Nonetheless, the Massachusetts Puritans set up rules of conduct for Puritan colonists that permitted the use of torture to force defendants to confess to crimes. Other colonies also allowed force to be used when interrogating (questioning) defendants. This reflected the common idea at the time that an accused person was guilty until proven innocent. Defendants were required to provide evidence of their innocence and had no right to remain silent before they did so.

On April 29, 1992, the jury—which included ten whites, one Filipino American, and one Latino, but no African Americans—acquitted the four police officers. The acquittals stunned many people who had seen the videotape. Within two hours, riots erupted in a predominantly African American South Central section of Los Angeles. The riots lasted seventy hours, leaving sixty people dead and more than two thousand injured. Order was restored through the combined efforts of the police, more than 10,000 National Guard troops, and 3,500 Army and Marine Corp troops.

In August of 1992 a federal grand jury indicted the four officers with violating King's civil rights. Koon was charged with depriving King of due process of law by failing to restrain the other officers. The other three officers were charged with violating King's right against unreasonable search and seizure because they had used unreasonable force during the arrest. The federal indictments did not violate the Double Jeopardy Clause because the dual sovereignty doctrine permits different government authorities to prosecute individuals for the same allegedly criminal acts.

At the federal trial, which was held in Los Angeles, the jury was more racially diverse than the one in Simi Valley: two jurors were African American, one was Latino, and the rest were white. This time King testified about the beating and charged that the officers had used racial epithets (abusive words). Observers agreed he was an effective witness. The videotape again was the central piece of evidence for both sides. On April 17, 1993, the jury convicted officers Koon and Powell of violating King's civil rights, but acquitted Wind and Briseno. Koon and Powell were sentenced to two-and-a-half years in prison.

By the time the states were deciding whether to ratify the Constitution, however, popular opposition to the use of torture led a number of states to include the privilege against self-incrimination in their state constitutions. Thus a number of the states asked Congress to include the same protection in the Bill of Rights, leading Madison to include the clause in the Fifth Amendment.

Under the Self-incrimination Clause the defendant is assumed to be innocent until proven guilty. Therefore the trial process is reversed. It is

**Fifth
Amendment**

*The group known as
the Hollywood Ten
were put in the
position of testifying
against themselves
and their colleagues
to spare themselves
from being stripped
of their rights.*

Reproduced by permission of
the Hearst Newspaper
Collection.

up to the government to prove a person guilty of a crime, and the defendant has no responsibility to help the government do this.

Protecting the innocent and the guilty

People sometimes assume a person who chooses to remain silent must be guilty. However, an innocent person may also exercise the right not to testify against him or herself. When an accused person chooses to remain silent, the prosecutor is not allowed to suggest that the defendant's silence means the person is guilty. And before the jurors begin to make their decision, the judge must tell them that the defendant's silence cannot be considered evidence of guilt.

Interrogations and forced confessions

The most common issue surrounding self-incrimination is how far police may go in questioning a suspect they have in custody. The Supreme Court first addressed this issue in 1897, in *Bram v. United States,* when it decided that a forced confession violates the Self-incrimination Clause. But deciding when a defendant has been forced to confess can be complicated.

THE VOLUNTARINESS TEST. In *Brown v. Mississippi* (1936) the Court established the voluntariness test for deciding when a confession could and could not be used in a trial. In the case, police had obtained confessions by brutally beating the suspects. The Supreme Court emphasized that a confession could not be used if circumstances suggested there was a good chance it was false.

There were problems with the voluntariness test. In order to decide whether a confession had been made voluntarily (willingly and without force) a court had to decide whether there had been any physical abuse or threats, whether there had been excessive questioning, or if the defendant had been denied the right to consult with a lawyer. The court also needed to determine if a defendant was capable of knowing his or her rights before making a confession. A person with a mental illness or with very little education, for example, may not be aware of his or her rights. But these facts were often open to interpretation, which made using the voluntariness test difficult in many cases.

In *Ashcraft v. Tennessee* (1944), for instance, the Court threw out a murder conviction because the defendant's confession came after thirty-six straight hours of police interrogation. The court called the lengthy period of questioning "inherently coercive." (In other words, for all practical purposes the police had forced the confession.) A month later in *Lyons v. Oklahoma,* however, the Court ruled that a defendant's confession had been voluntary, even though the police forced the defendant to sit for twelve hours with the bones of murder victims sitting on a pan in his lap.

THE RIGHT TO AN ATTORNEY. In *Escobedo v. Illinois* (1964), the Supreme Court broke away from the voluntariness test. In the case, police obtained a confession after refusing the defendant's repeated requests to consult with his attorney. The Court ruled that once a suspect has been taken into custody "if the suspect has requested and been denied an opportunity to consult with his lawyer and the police have not effectively warned him of his absolute constitutional right to remain silent" then nothing the defendant said to the police, voluntarily or not, can be used against him in a trial.

THE *MIRANDA* WARNING. *Escobedo* made it clear that police departments had to ensure that the Self-incrimination Clause was more than words on paper. But in 1966 the Supreme Court went a step further.

Ernesto Miranda was arrested in 1963 and taken to the police station where witnesses identified him as a rapist. Police then interrogated

Miranda without telling him he had the right to an attorney. Miranda confessed and was later convicted of rape and kidnapping. However, in *Miranda v. Arizona* (1966), he appealed his conviction to the Supreme Court, arguing that he had never been advised of his legal rights.

In looking at the case, the Court noted that most police did not use methods such as beating suspects or denying them their rights. Nonetheless, the Court said, such methods were common enough to merit widespread concern. As a result, the Court established certain procedures that police departments are required to follow when taking a person into custody.

These procedures, known as Miranda warnings, entail informing a person being interrogated of their rights, including:

- The right to remain silent.

It is now mandatory that all police read a suspect his or her Miranda rights upon arresting them.

- The right to invoke Fifth Amendment protection against self-incrimination at *anytime* during an interrogation.
- The right to have a lawyer present during interrogation.
- The right to have an attorney appointed if they cannot afford one.

WARNING

The constitution requires that I inform you of your rights:

You have a right to remain silent. If you talk to any police officer, anything you say can and will be used against you in court.

You have a right to consult with a lawyer before you are questioned, and may have him with you during questioning.

If you cannot afford a lawyer, one will be appointed for you, if you wish, before any questioning.

If you wish to answer questions, you have the right to stop answering at any time.

You may stop answering questions at any time if you wish to talk to a lawyer, and may have him with you during any further questioning.

Rev. 9-79

- The fact that anything the person says can and will be used against him or her in court.

The Court ruled that statements made by a suspect who was in police custody would not be admissible in a trial unless the suspect had been fully informed of his or her rights and had then voluntarily waived (given up) those rights. Since 1966 the *Miranda* warning has become a routine part of police work.

At first, many people feared that the Miranda warnings would interfere with police work. The Court pointed out, however, that interrogations were still a perfectly legitimate tool, as long as a person knew his or her rights and was allowed to exercise them. Reading the Miranda warnings has also kept defendants from later trying to take back their confessions, since after the warning has been given, anything a suspect says can be used in court. (see "Limits to the Self-incrimination Clause" box.)

The Due Process Clause

The Due Process Clause in the Fifth Amendment states that no person shall be "deprived of life, liberty, or property, without due process of law." Established under English common law (legal tradition), due process requires government legal proceedings to be fair and is broken down into two major categories: procedural due process and substantive due process.

Procedural due process limits the actions the government can take to enforce its laws. The government may not start legal proceedings against someone without first notifying that person. Furthermore, the government must provide an opportunity for the person to speak on his or her own behalf before it can hand out any type of punishment. Under procedural due process, a person must be informed when he or she is being put on trial and must also be given a chance to testify during the trial.

Substantive due process prohibits the creation of laws that unreasonably restrict a person's substantive (essential) rights. Under this type of due process, for instance, a law that took away a person's right to free speech (see chapter one) would not be allowed.

There are two due process clauses in the Constitution. The Fifth Amendment clause was created to limit the actions of the federal government. There is also a Due Process Clause in the Fourteenth Amendment (see chapter fourteen) that applies to state and local governments. Since the late 1800s most due process cases heard by the Supreme Court have

**Fifth
Amendment**

LIMITS TO THE SELF-INCRIMINATION CLAUSE

The right against self-incrimination is not absolute. A person may not refuse to file an income tax return on Fifth Amendment grounds or fail to report a hit-and-run accident. The government may compel defendants to provide fingerprints, blood and hair samples, voice exemplars, and writing samples without violating the right against self-incrimination because such evidence is used for the purpose of identification and is not considered testimony. And defendants may not refuse to stand in a police lineup. The Supreme Court has even placed limits on the protection against self-incrimination offered by the *Miranda* decision (see "The Self-incrimination Clause").

The "public safety exception," for example, allows police to ask certain questions without reading the suspect the Miranda warnings, when the "threat to the public safety outweighs (the) ... privilege against self-incrimination." For instance, an officer may determine the location of a gun or other weapon while arresting someone before advising the suspect of his or her rights. Any weapons found because of this line of questioning can be used in a trial.

Another exception is the "inevitable discovery exception." This allows police to use evidence found because of an unusable confession when it can be shown they would have found the evidence without the confession. In the case of *Nix v. Williams* (1984), for instance, a murder

centered on the Fourteenth Amendment. However, the clauses in both amendments have had a close legal relationship in the courts.

Making government follow the rules

The Supreme Court first looked closely at procedural due process in *Murray's Lessee v. Hoboken Land and Improvement Co.* (1856). In that case the Court set up standards for judging whether particular government actions followed due process.

At issue in the case was the government's method of collecting debts from citizens who owed the government money. The Court used two principles to decide whether the government's process for debt collection was following due process. First, the court said that the process

suspect was repeatedly refused the right to consult with an attorney. Eventually he agreed to lead police to the body of his victim anyway. The Supreme Court ruled that since an ongoing police search in the area would have discovered the body, it could be used as evidence even though the suspect's rights had been violated.

Confessions that are the result of "non-custodial interrogations" also do not require the use of Miranda warnings. If a person is not under arrest or in police custody and voluntarily confesses to the police without being read the Miranda warnings, the confession is still admissible in court.

On February 8, 1999, a three-judge panel of the Fourth Circuit Court of Appeals issued a ruling that declared *Miranda* invalid. In *U.S. v. Dickerson,* the court found that Congress had passed a law in 1968 that legally overturned (threw out) the Supreme Court's *Miranda* ruling. The 1968 statute allows confessions made voluntarily to be admitted in court. This would seem to allow confessions made by defendants who have not been formally informed of their rights to be used against them.

This ruling has proven very controversial and currently only applies to the states under the jurisdiction (authority) of the Fourth Circuit Court: Maryland, North Carolina, South Carolina, Virginia, and West Virginia. It is assumed, however, that the Supreme Court will likely review the case because it is in direct conflict with the law in every other part of the country.

must not conflict with any of the terms set out in the Constitution. (For instance, did the process take away the debtor's right to free speech?) Second, the process must not conflict with English common law, which the Court viewed as directly connected to American legal tradition.

In the *Murray's Lessee* case, the Court found that the English government had historically used the same methods for collecting debts in England as the American government was now using and therefore the procedure followed due process.

However, in *Hurtado v. California* (1884) the Supreme Court ruled that if due process of law was limited to include only traditional procedures, then the legal system would be "incapable of progress or improvement." Instead, the Court ruled that any legal proceeding that preserves

DUE PROCESS AND DRUG PROPERTY SEIZURES

The law allows the federal government to seize any property that is used to commit a federal drug offense. However, critics of these laws argue that many of these seizures violate the Fifth Amendment's Due Process Clause. In the case of *United States v. Good* (1993) the Supreme Court agreed with the critics, ruling that the government must give notice and a court hearing to people before seizing their property.

In 1985 Hawaii police officers searched the home of James Good and discovered eighty-nine pounds of marijuana. Good pleaded guilty to a state drug charge and was sentenced to one year in jail and five years' probation. In 1989 the federal government decided to seize Good's house and property since it had been used to commit a federal drug crime. (The Supreme Court's "dual sovereignty" doctrine allows separate state and federal punishments for certain actions; see "The Double Jeopardy Clause".) During a hearing in which Good was not present, a federal court judge concluded that the government could take Good's property.

Good argued that the seizure deprived him of his property without due process of law since he was not given a chance to state his side of the case. The Supreme Court agreed, citing the Fifth Amendment's guarantee that no person shall "be deprived of life, liberty, or property, without due process of law." The Court ruled that individuals must receive notice of the government's intentions, as well as an opportunity to be heard at a hearing before the government deprives them of property.

the "principles of liberty and justice, must be held to be a due process of law" regardless of whether it was new or old.

Substantive due process

The first major cases to involve the issue of substantive due process concerned the Fourteenth Amendment's Due Process Clause, which relates to the actions of state governments. In the 1897 case of *Allgeyer v. Louisiana* the Court found that a Louisiana law that limited the types of contracts people could enter into with out-of-state insurance firms was unconstitutional, because it deprived people of their right to enter into lawful contracts.

Later, in *Lochner v. New York* (1905), the Supreme Court ruled that a New York law that limited the number of hours bakers could work (for health reasons) violated the worker's freedom to make legal contracts. (see chapter fourteen.)

Both of these cases used the Fourteenth Amendment's due process clause to strike down state laws. In *Adair v. United States* (1908), however, the court used the Fifth Amendment's Due Process Clause to strike down a federal law against "yellow dog" contracts. These contracts required workers to promise never to join a union. (A union is a group of workers who come together to bargain or negotiate with an employer.) At the time such yellow dog contracts were commonly used to prevent unions from forming.

The Supreme Court struck down the anti-yellow dog law, as well as a law that set a minimum wage for female workers in the District of Columbia. In both cases the Court ruled that employers and employees had a substantive right to negotiate whatever terms they pleased, and that the government could not intrude on these rights without violating the Fifth Amendment's Due Process Clause.

During the Great Depression (a period of severe economic hardship that lasted from the Stock Market crash of 1929 through the end of the 1930s), however, the Court abandoned its opposition to all government regulation of business. In the case of *West Coast Hotel Co. v. Parrish* (1937), the Court allowed a law requiring employers to pay a minimum wage to their workers to remain in effect. In that case the Court stated that society requires protection "against the evils which menace the health, safety, morals, and welfare of the people." Therefore, when government regulation is reasonable and furthers the interests of society as a whole, it can be said to follow due process.

The Court has used the concept of substantive due process to strike down any number of state and federal laws that unreasonably deprive people of their constitutional rights. For example, the Court has established that there is a substantive right to privacy derived from the First, Fourth, and Ninth Amendments (see chapters one, four, and nine). In *Griswold v. State of Connecticut* (1965), the Court struck down a state law which prohibited the use of contraception (birth control), even by married couples. Using a substantive due process test, the Court ruled that the law unreasonably limited people's right to privacy.

Fifth Amendment

Adding equal protection to the Fifth Amendment

In addition to its due process clause, the Fourteenth Amendment includes a so-called equal protection clause that says that state governments may not "deny to any person the equal protection of the laws." Taken together, these two clauses mean that due process requires the government to treat everyone equally under the law.

The Fifth Amendment does not include such an equal protection clause. But in the case of *Bolling v. Sharpe* (1954), the Supreme Court concluded that the Due Process Clause contained in the Fourteenth Amendment (which only applied to states) was a better protection against unfairness than the Fifth Amendment's Due Pro-

There are some exceptions to the equal protection of the Fifth Amendment. Defendants of a military court martial are not protected against having to testify against themselves. Reproduced by permission of AP/Wide World Photos.

cess Clause (which applied to the federal government). With this is mind, the Court said that it would be "unthinkable" for the Constitution to require more from the states than it required of the federal government. Thus, the Court ruled that guaranteeing "equal protection under the law" was, in fact, part of due process, and therefore was part of the Fifth Amendment's Due Process Clause.

Since *Bolling* the Supreme Court has used the equal protection reading of the Fifth Amendment to strike down a number of federal laws, such as those that discriminate against on the basis of a person's gender (sex).

The Eminent Domain Clause

The Eminent Domain Clause states that private property shall not "be taken for public use, without just compensation." In effect this clause establishes the government's right to take a person's property for public use—such as building a road or a school—while requiring the government to pay owners a fair price for any "taken" property.

Before the American Revolutionary War, it was customary for the colonial governments to take private property for public use without paying the owner anything. Usually, the government seized undeveloped land for the purpose of building roads and developing the frontier (unsettled land).

After the Revolution began, American forces often seized property (especially from colonists who were loyal to Great Britain) for military use, often without making any compensation to the owner. In both cases giving up private property for the common good was seen as part of the public duty of every colonist.

Many people, though, were upset by these practices and felt that individual property rights should not always be sacrificed for the good of society. Thus the Eminent Domain Clause was crafted to balance the public's interests with individual owners' property rights.

A constitutional first

The clauses in the Fifth Amendment were originally designed to apply only to the federal government. This meant that state governments had the right to take private property without paying the owner. However, the passage of the Fourteenth Amendment in 1868 changed that decision. The first section of the Fourteenth Amendment states that "No State shall make or enforce any law which shall abridge [lessen] the privileges or immunities of citizens of the United States; nor shall any State deprive any person of life, liberty, or property, without due process of law." (see chapter fourteen.) This meant that state governments could not make laws that took away rights that were given to them by the federal government.

In *Chicago, Burlington, & Quincy Railroads v. Chicago (1897)* the court ruled that this section of the Fourteenth Amendment required state governments to make fair payments for any property they took, just as the federal government was required to. This ruling marked the first time that the Supreme Court used the Fourteenth Amendment to expand the reach of the Bill of Rights to state governments.

**Fifth
Amendment**

*It is legal for the
government to seize
private property,
as long as the
government follows
the standards of
due process.*

Reproduced by permission
of AP/Wide World Photos.

Defining the terms of Eminent Domain

The Eminent Domain Clause does not define what types of "public use" justify a taking of private property, nor does the clause specify how to determine what "just compensation" (a fair price) is.

PUBLIC USE. To determine whether property can be taken, the courts must first decide whether use of the property will benefit the public. The definition of public use has broadened over the years to include such things as trade centers, municipal civic centers, and airport expansions. The Supreme Court has even declared that improving the physical appearance of an area constitutes a legitimate public use. In *Berman v. Parker* (1954), for instance, the justices ruled that slums could be cleared to make the city more attractive.

JUST COMPENSATION. There is no set formula for determining the fair price for taken property. Compensation (payment) is generally set at the price an owner could reasonably expect to get from a person who wished to buy the property for private use. However, the amount paid should be based on the owner's loss, not the government's gain. For example, if an owner could expect to receive twenty thousand dollars from a private

buyer, this sum will determine the amount paid for the property, even if the government plans to build a civic center on the property that will generate millions of dollars in business.

When regulation becomes taking

The government often passes laws that regulate (control) the way property owners can use their land in order to serve public interests such as protecting the environment. Usually these regulations are not considered a taking of property. However, in some cases a regulation reduces the value of the property so severely that the government may pay the owner some compensation.

The Supreme Court first examined this issue in *Pennsylvania Coal Co. v. Mahon* (1922), when it ruled that a Pennsylvania law that prevented coal mining on certain types of property hurt the coal company that had rights to mine the land. The Court decided that the statute constituted a taking and that the state must pay the coal company just compensation. The Court ruled that "while property may be regulated to a certain extent, if regulation goes too far it will be recognized as a taking."

The Supreme Court confronted a similar issue in *Lucas v. South Carolina Coastal Council* (1992). In 1986 David Lucas purchased two residential lots near the beach in South Carolina. Lucas paid nine hundred seventy-five thousand dollars for the lots, on which he planned to build two single-family homes. When Lucas bought the property, the South Carolina government did require that he get special permission to build homes on the land. But in 1988 South Carolina enacted a law that prohibited building new houses too close to the beachfront. The law was intended to fight the problem of beach erosion (beaches were washing away due to over development). Because of the law Lucas was not allowed to build houses on his property.

The U.S. Supreme Court ruled that the right to erect a house is an "essential use of the land" that came with the purchase of the property. In its ruling the Court stated that if Lucas reasonably could have expected to build on his property before the law was passed, then the law effectively took away his property rights, and South Carolina would have to pay compensation.

Summing Up the Parts of the Fifth Amendment

Taken together, the five clauses of the Fifth help define a person's rights when engaged in direct legal proceedings against the government. Each

**Fifth
Amendment**

of the Fifth Amendment's clauses provides a specific type of protection against government abuses of the legal system. Individuals had claimed these rights in England and America before, but in both places the government often ignored them. As part of the Bill of Rights, the Fifth Amendment firmly established these protections within the legal fabric of the United States.

For More Information

Books

Fireside, Harvey. *The Fifth Amendment: The Right to Remain Silent.* Springfield, NJ: Enslow Publishers, 1998.

Hyde, Henry. *Forfeiting Our Property Rights: Is Your Property Safe from Seizure?* Washington, D.C.: Cato Institute, 1995.

Kronenwetter, Michael. *The Supreme Court of the United States.* Springfield, NJ: Enslow Publishers, 1996.

Landau, Elaine. *Your Legal Rights: From Custody Battles to School Searches—The Headline Making Cases that Affect Your Life.* New York: Walter and Company, 1995.

Lawson, Don. "The Miranda Case and Its Aftermath" in *Landmark Supreme Court Cases.* Springfield, NJ: Enslow Publishers, 1987.

Riley, Gale Blasser. *Miranda v. Arizona: Right of the Accused.* Springfield, NJ: Enslow Publishers, 1994.

Wice, Paul B. *Miranda v. Arizona.* New York: Franklin Watts, 1996.

Web Sites

FindLaw Internet Legal Resources. *The Fifth Amendment and Annotations.* [Online] http://caselaw.findlaw.com/data/constitution/amendment05/01.html (accessed January 24, 2001).

FindLaw Internet Legal Resources. *U.S. Supreme Court Opinions.* [Online] http://www.findlaw.com/casecode/supreme.html (accessed January 24, 2001).

"Legal Survival Guide: What Is the Miranda Warning?" *Court TV Online.* [Online] http://www.courttv.com/legalhelp/lawguide/criminal/91.html (accessed January 24, 2001).

Sources

Books

Encyclopedia of World Biography. 17 vols. Detroit: Gale Research, 1998.

Hall, Kermit L. *The Magic Mirror.* New York: Oxford University Press, 1989.

Hall, Kermit L., ed. *Oxford Companion to the Supreme Court of the United States.* New York: Oxford University Press, 1992.

Israel, Jerold H., and Wayne R. LaFave. *Criminal Procedure in a Nutshell.* St. Paul, MN.: West Publishing Co., 1993.

Stephens, Otis H., Jr., and John M. Scheb II. *American Constitutional Law.* St. Paul, MN.: West Publishing, 1993.

West's Encyclopedia of American Law 12 vols. St. Paul, MN.: West Group, 1997.

Wright, Robert R. *Land Use in a Nutshell.* St. Paul, MN.: West Publishing, 1994.

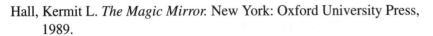

**Fifth
Amendment**

The Sixth Amendment

In all criminal prosecutions, the accused shall enjoy the right to a speedy and public trial, by an impartial jury of the State and district wherein the crime shall have been committed, which district shall have been previously ascertained by law, and to be informed of the nature and cause of the accusation; to be confronted with the witnesses against him; to have compulsory process for obtaining witnesses in his favor, and to have the Assistance of Counsel for his defence [sic].

Like the Fifth Amendment, the Sixth Amendment is made up of a series of clauses, or individual phrases that each define a particular set of rights. Along with several of the Fifth Amendment clauses (see chapter five), the Sixth Amendment establishes specific rights for those accused of criminal actions by the government.

Under the Sixth Amendment, a person who is accused of a crime by the government has the right to know what they have been accused of and why. Once accused, the defendant has the right to a lawyer. If the accused cannot afford a lawyer, the government must provide one.

A defendant also has the right to a trial by jury. A jury is a group of citizens who listen to evidence and decide whether the defendant is guilty or innocent. A person's trial must start quickly and must be open to the public, and jury members cannot have made up their minds about the case before the trial starts.

A defendant also has the right to face and question the prosecution's witnesses as well as to call witnesses of his or her own.

These rights are contained in specific clauses within the Sixth Amendment that ensure:

- The right to a speedy and public trial.

RATIFICATION FACTS

PROPOSED: Submitted by Congress to the states: September 25, 1789, along with the other nine amendments that comprise the Bill of Rights.

RATIFICATION: Ratified by the required three-fourths of states (eleven of fourteen): December 15, 1791. Declared to be part of the Constitution: December 15, 1791.

RATIFYING STATES: New Jersey, November 20, 1789; Maryland, December 19, 1789; North Carolina, December 22, 1789; South Carolina, January 19, 1790; New Hampshire, January 25, 1790; Delaware, January 28, 1790; New York, February 24, 1790; Pennsylvania, March 10, 1790; Rhode Island, June 7, 1790; Vermont, November 3, 1791; Virginia, December 15, 1791 (amendment adopted).

- The right to trial by an impartial (unprejudiced) jury.
- The right to know the nature and cause of an accusation.
- The right to be confronted with the witnesses against him or her.
- The right to compulsory process, which requires witnesses called by a defendant to appear in court.
- The right to assistance of counsel, which allows defendants to obtain help in presenting their side of the case.

Origins of the Sixth Amendment

Many of the rights embodied in the Sixth Amendment can be traced to English common law (legal traditions). Trial by jury, the assistance of counsel, and the right to a speedy trial all existed in some form in England before they were transported to England's colonies in America.

English criminal trials before the twelfth century took place in forms that seem odd to modern observers. For instance, in "trial by battle" persons accused of a crime would battle their accusers to determine who "won" the case. These fights were "refereed" by robed judges. Another English tradition that predates jury trials was the "trial by

ordeal." In these trials defendants were forced to undergo potentially life-ending ordeals, such as walking across red-hot metal or being thrown in a river with hands and feet bound up, to decide their fates. Needless to say, even innocent defendants did not fare well in such trials.

A lopsided judicial system

By the middle of the twelfth century trials routinely called upon the oldest and most respected people from a defendant's neighborhood to testify at his or her trial and even decide the outcome of the trial. Such

Before there were jury trials, there were trials by ordeal, which forced defendants to perform death-defying feats to decide their fates.
Reproduced by permission of Archive Photos, Inc.

groups of local citizen-witnesses were some of the earliest juries. Impartial jury verdicts, however, were still in short supply. In fact, the government often fined or punished jurors who found a defendant not guilty. This situation did not change until 1670, when public outrage over *Bushell's Case*—in which a juror was jailed for finding a defendant innocent—at last put an end to such punishments.

Judicial rights in colonial America

American colonists enjoyed many rights that their English counterparts did not. Each colony settled during the seventeenth century included safeguards of personal liberty in its written laws. West New Jersey established a set of fundamental laws in 1676 that guaranteed a public trial by a jury of twelve "good and lawful men." Likewise, the Pennsylvania Frame of Government Charter (1683) included the right to have justice speedily administered by a jury of twelve men. And though paid lawyers were originally frowned upon in the colonies, as states began using professional prosecutors in court, it became common in the colonies for defendants to hire professional lawyers to plead their cases.

Judicial rights after the Revolutionary War

War broke out between Great Britain and its American colonies in 1775, in large part because colonists felt that the British government had repeatedly violated their rights. By the time they won their independence from the British Empire in 1781, most of the thirteen original colonies had adopted bills of rights that included the right to trial by jury.

Under the Articles of Confederation, ratified in 1781, the newly independent states formed a weak union in which most governmental power was kept by the states. By 1788, however, the states adopted the United States Constitution (see Introduction), establishing a strong national government with power divided among an executive branch headed by the president, Congress (the legislative or law-making body of government), and the Supreme Court.

Madison writes and promotes amendments

The right to a jury trial was included in the new Constitution, which states that "the Trial of all Crimes, except in cases of impeachment, shall be by Jury." But many people worried that the Constitution did not do enough to ensure the people's rights and pushed for a national bill of rights to be added to the Constitution.

James Madison (1751–1836), a member of the House of Representatives from Virginia who later became the fourth president of the United States, spent much of his first session in Congress writing and promoting amendment proposals that eventually became the Bill of Rights (see Introduction). Among these proposals was a proposal for an amendment ensuring the rights of the accused in criminal trials, which was nearly identical to the final wording of the Sixth Amendment. After some minor changes, the Amendment was passed by Congress in 1789 and adopted by the states with the other Bill of Rights amendments in 1791.

Interpreting the Sixth Amendment

Much of the Sixth Amendment is open to broad interpretation. For example, does the right to assistance of counsel mean that a defendant is *allowed* to have a lawyer's assistance? Or does it *guarantee* defendants the right to an attorney even if they cannot afford one? Similar questions may be asked about many of the Sixth Amendment's clauses.

Under the Constitution, the ultimate power to decide such questions belongs to the Supreme Court of the United States, the highest court in the land. The Supreme Court often makes decisions regarding questions and issues that arise in lower court cases. Over the years, the Supreme Court's decisions in cases involving a defendant's Sixth Amendment rights have defined and redefined exactly what those rights are.

Equal protection and due process

Depending on the crime and where it took place, criminal trials in the United States may be held at either the federal or state level. Most armed robberies, for instance, are state crimes and are tried in state courts. But bank robbery is a federal crime that is tried in federal court.

Originally, protections offered by the Bill of Rights amendments applied only at the federal level. Individual state governments were not required to abide by them. It was possible in a state trial, for instance, for a person to be denied the right to counsel or even to a jury trial. But with the ratification of the Fourteenth Amendment (see chapter fourteen) in 1868, that began to change. The Fourteenth Amendment's equal protection and due process clauses established the idea that all citizens must be treated equally under federal *and* state laws. Over the years the Supreme Court has used the Fourteenth Amendment to require the states to comply with the Bill of Rights. This process, however, has been slow, and it was not until the 1960s that the Supreme Court began extending Sixth Amendment rights to defendants in state trials.

A speedy trial

Speedy justice was especially important in colonial times, when defendants were sometimes forced to travel all the way to England to stand trial. But even today, a defendant may wish to have a case settled as soon as possible in order to clear his or her reputation. A speedy trial also ensures that a defendant is not kept in police custody any longer than necessary.

The definition of "speedy" is open to interpretation. The Supreme Court first addressed the Speedy Trial Clause in *Beavers v. Haubert* (1905). In that case a defendant faced criminal charges in New York and in the District of Columbia, and the New York court allowed the District of Columbia court to hold its trial first. The defendant argued that his right to a speedy trial in New York was being obstructed. The Supreme Court held that each case must be judged on its own circumstances. Since the delay in this case was caused by another trial, the Court ruled that the public's right to try the defendant for both crimes outweighed the defendant's right to a swift trial in New York.

The court considers four factors when deciding if a defendant's right to a swift trial has been violated:

- The length of the delay: If the delay is found to be sufficiently long the court will then consider the other factors.

- The reason for the delay: If there is a good reason for the delay, the court may decide that a speedy trial was not possible.

- Whether the defendant asked for a swift trial: If a defendant agrees to or causes delays in the trial, then the right to a swift trial is not violated.

- Was any prejudice caused by the delay: Was the defendant hurt by the delay? If the court finds that a delay did not cause the defendant harm, a trial may be allowed to proceed.

If it is determined that the government has unnecessarily delayed the case for an unreasonable amount of time, the charges against a defendant must be dropped. In 1967 the Supreme Court applied the Speedy Trial Clause of the Sixth Amendment to the states in *Klopfer v. North Carolina.* In that case a defendant in North Carolina was accused of a criminal trespass. When a jury in the trial was unable to decide the case,

Sixth Amendment

**Sixth
Amendment**

*In some court cases
where the public is
excluded, courtroom
artists may draw
illustrations of what
went on during the
proceeding.* Reproduced
by permission of AP/Wide
World Photos.

the government prosecutor dismissed the charge but retained the right to charge the defendant again at any time.

The defendant argued that this violated his right to a speedy trial. The Supreme Court agreed, finding that keeping the defendant under a cloud of suspicion for an indefinite period of time violated the Sixth Amendment. On the other hand, the Court found in *Barker v. Wingo* (1972) that a defendant had given up his right to a speedy trial because he had objected to the government's first eleven requests to delay his trial.

United States v. McDonald (1982) involved a highly publicized case of an Army doctor charged with murdering his wife and two daughters. The Army dismissed the charges in 1970, but the case was later taken up by the U.S. Department of Justice, which continued to investigate the matter. In 1975 the defendant was indicted and later convicted of the crimes. After the conviction, the defendant argued that his right to a speedy trial had been violated. However, the Supreme Court ruled that since the defendant "was not under arrest, not in custody" and had not been formally indicted, he was "legally and constitutionally" in the same position as if no charges had been made up to that point. In other words, his right to a speedy trial did not begin until his indictment in 1975.

A public trial

By guaranteeing the right to a public trial, in which the public is allowed to attend court proceedings against an individual, the Sixth Amendment is designed to increase public confidence in the justice system. In the case of *In re Oliver* (1948), the Supreme Court found that the right to a public trial is "a safeguard against any attempt to employ our courts as instruments of persecution"—that is, it serves as a protection against the government abusing its judicial power.

There are, nonetheless, limits on the right to a public trial. Courts may temporarily exclude the public from a trial when a witness might be embarrassed by the public's presence, or in order to protect the identity of an undercover agent. A court may also limit the number of spectators or throw out spectators who are disruptive.

Still, courts cannot abuse their power to exclude spectators. In *Waller v. Georgia,* a Georgia court had agreed to close a part of a trial to protect the privacy of one of the witnesses. However, the trial remained closed to the public for seven days, during which time less than three hours were spent on issues that involved the witness's privacy. The Supreme Court ruled that the closed trial violated the defendant's Sixth Amendment right to a public trial, finding that a "closure must be no broader than necessary."

The Jury System

The main purpose of a jury trial is to prevent governmental abuse by placing ordinary citizens between the government and the accused. The Supreme Court put it this way: "[T]he purpose of trial by jury is to prevent oppression by the Government by providing a safeguard against" the abuse of power by judges or prosecutors. By giving a relatively large group of people from the community the final decision-making power in a trial, jury trials help prevent judges or prosecutors from abusing their power.

The original Constitution required that all criminal cases be tried by a jury. But the Sixth Amendment's jury clause goes farther, requiring trial by an *impartial* jury. In order to ensure a fair trial, it is important that a jury is not biased or prejudiced against a defendant before the trial begins. In other words, jurors should not have made up their minds about a case before hearing the facts.

Sixth Amendment

Picking a jury

Making sure a jury is impartial is not easy. At the start of a trial, a large group of potential jurors is called together by the court. From this large group the defense and prosecution lawyers go about choosing the final jury. During the selection process, attorneys from both sides may ask the group members questions and may then ask the judge to exclude certain members from the jury for various reasons.

But a court may put limits on who is excluded and for what reasons. In *Connors v. United States* (1895) the defendant essentially asked potential jurors what political party they belonged to. The judge in the case stopped this line of questioning, saying that such information was not relevant to the case. The Supreme Court agreed with the trial judge, ruling that a juror's "political convictions" would not necessarily prevent him or her from seeking a fair verdict.

The selection process, however, is different for every trial, and judges and attorneys may have to take any number of circumstances into consideration while attempting to select an impartial jury.

Though the Supreme Court ruled that six-member juries are legitimate, in *Ballew v. Georgia* (1978) the Court found that "the purpose and functioning of the jury in a criminal trial is seriously impaired ... by a reduction in size to below six members."

The Court threw out another of the "essential elements" outlined in *Patton* in a 1972 ruling. In the case of *Apodaca v. Oregon* (1972) the justices held that the Constitution does not require a unanimous verdict in state criminal trials; they added that the essential element of a jury trial is to put the "common sense judgement" of a group of citizens between "the accused and his accuser." This purpose, according to the Court, does not require a unanimous verdict. In *Burch v. Louisiana* (1979), however, the Supreme Court ruled that when a six-person jury is used, a unanimous verdict is required to convict a defendant.

Despite the Supreme Court's rulings that neither the unanimous verdict nor the twelve-person jury is required by the Constitution, only a handful of states have done away with either of these centuries-old common law traditions.

IN THE NEWS. Newspapers and other media (such as television and radio) often cover criminal cases before they come to trial, and it is possible for negative pretrial publicity to influence potential jurors against a defendant before a trial begins.

The treason case of Aaron Burr (1756–1836) in 1807 was one of the first cases in the United States to be widely covered in the press. Burr, a former U.S. vice president, was accused of plotting to take over Texas and establish the area as an independent nation. The defense claimed that the Sixth Amendment guaranteed Burr a trial by a jury "perfectly indifferent and free from prejudice"—in other words, a jury made up of jurors who had never heard of the case. Of course, this would have been nearly impossible with such a high-profile case. The Supreme Court ruled that such a perfect standard was unobtainable and that as long as the jurors were "open to a fair consideration," they could be considered impartial. In some instances, however, jurors who have strong opinions about a defendant based on media coverage of a case may be excluded from the jury.

WORKING FOR UNCLE SAM? Until 1936, the Supreme Court held that government employees could not be impartial jurors in federal criminal cases, since they worked for the same employer as the prosecution. But in *United States v. Wood* (1936) the Court ruled that there was no historical basis for a ban on government employees as jurors in criminal cases. Since that ruling, government employees have not been automatically excluded from serving as jurors.

EXCLUDING PREJUDICE–SOMETIMES. Depending on the circumstances of a case, a juror's prejudice against a certain race, religion, or nationality may be used to exclude him or her from a jury. But it must first be shown that such prejudice is relevant to the case.

For example, in *Ham v. South Carolina,* (1973), a well-known black civil rights activist claimed that he had been framed on drug charges because of his civil rights work. At his trial, Ham had not been allowed to ask potential jurors about their racial prejudice, and the Supreme Court found that this kept him from receiving a fair trial.

In the 1976 *Ristaino v. Ross* case, however, the Court held that a defendant is not entitled to inquire specifically about racial prejudice dur-

Sometimes, the news coverage of a particular case may make it difficult for the court to find impartial people to serve on the jury.

Reproduced by permission of AP/Wide World Photos.

The treason case of Aaron Burr was one of the first cases in the United States to be widely covered in the press. Courtesy of the Library of Congress.

ing jury selection just because a case involves a conflict between individuals of different race or ethnic origin. The Court pointed out that the *Ham* case was special because "[r]acial issues ... were inextricably bound up" in that trial.

A CROSS-SECTION OF THE COMMUNITY. In *Taylor v. Louisiana* (1975) the Supreme Court ruled that a jury system in Louisiana, which excluded women from serving on juries, deprived a defendant of his Sixth Amendment right to an impartial jury. According to the Court, an impartial jury can only be achieved if it is taken from a pool that is representative of the entire community and does not exclude certain groups in the community.

This cross-section requirement does not mean that the final jury must mirror the community. It simply means that no one group, whether it be a certain race, or gender, or can be systematically excluded from the pool of potential jurors.

DEATH PENALTY VIEWS. Some crimes may be punished by death. These capital crimes require jurors not only to decide a defendant's guilt but also to decide whether or not to impose the death penalty. In death penalty cases the Supreme Court has ruled that the prosecution may exclude potential jurors if they admit they are strongly opposed to *any* use of the death penalty. Similarly, the defense may excuse potential jurors who say they would *automatically* impose the death penalty if the defendant were convicted.

Sixth Amendment

Being called to be on a jury can sometimes mean only a few hours of commitment, or many days or weeks of commitment.

Accusation and Confrontation

The Sixth Amendment requires the government to inform a defendant of the "nature and cause of the accusation" against him or her and allow the defendant to "to be confronted with the witnesses against him." Both of these clauses are intended to keep the government from using "secret charges" or secret witnesses to prosecute a defendant and help the accused prepare his or her defense.

Informing a person of the nature and cause of an accusation means telling a defendant what he or she is accused of and on why. For the most part, defendants are informed of the charges against them when they are indicted (formally charged by a grand jury or a hearing). The Supreme Court ruled in *Cruikshank v. United States* (1875) that simply informing a defendant that he or she is accused of "armed robbery" or "kidnapping" is not sufficient. An indictment must also provide details—such as where and when the crime took place and what evidence the prosecutor is basing the charges on—to put the defendant on "proper notice."

In *Rosen v. United States* (1896) the Supreme Court ruled that an indictment must contain a detailed enough description of the charges to enable a defendant to "make his defense." Such a specific description of the crime also provides defendants with a tool to avoid later prosecutions for the same crime. (see "The Double Jeopardy Clause" section in chapter five.)

The right to cross-examine

The right of an accused to be "confronted with the witnesses against him" gives a defendant the right to be present during his or her trial and to cross-examine (question) the witnesses called against him or her. This clause prevents the government from simply asking questions that help convict the defendant while ignoring questions that might help him or her.

Along with the Compulsory Process Clause (see section below), which allows the defendant to call his or her own witnesses, the Confrontation Clause provides the defendant with an important tool to counter the prosecution's charges.

The right of confrontation also give the defendant the right to be present at nearly all points in the trial process, beginning with jury selection until the verdict is announced. If a defendant cannot understand English, the court must find a way (such as providing a professional translator) for the defendant to understand and cross-examine witnesses.

WHERE'S THE WITNESS? In the case of *Motes v. United States* (1900) the government was responsible for the absence of one of its own witnesses. Since the witness was unavailable, the government wanted to introduce a transcript (written copy) of the witness's testimony from a pretrial hearing.

The Supreme Court ruled that since the witness's absence was the government's fault, and "was not attributable to the actions or influence of the accused" the testimony could not be used, since the defendant did not have the opportunity to cross-examine.

DYING TO BE HEARD. A witness's absence does not always violate the defendant's right to confrontation. In the case of *Mattox v. United States* (1895) the Supreme Court allowed a transcript of testimony from one trial to be used in another trial of the same defendant. Two witnesses had died between the accused's first trial and his second. Partly because the defendant had been given the opportunity to cross-examine the witnesses in the earlier trial, the Supreme Court ruled that the transcripts of the dead witnesses' testimony could be used.

REMOVING THE DEFENDANT FROM COURT. Defendant's may also forfeit (lose) their right to confrontation. In *Illinois v. Allen* (1970) the Supreme Court ruled that a trial judge had the right to remove a defendant from his own trial for repeatedly disrupting the courtroom. The Court ruled that the removal was reasonable and that the defendant could regain his right to confront his accusers simply by agreeing not to disrupt the proceedings.

PROTECTING MINORS. Protecting young victims of sexual abuse from having to face an alleged attacker presents a challenge to the Confrontation Clause. The Court decided that an Iowa law that allowed a child to testify

Every defendant has the right to be present in the courtroom to see his or her accuser being cross-examined by an attorney. Reproduced by permission of AP/Wide World Photos.

behind a screen, blocking the view of the defendant, was unconstitutional in *Coy v. Iowa* (1988). In another instance, however, the Court ruled that a Maryland law that allowed a child to testify in a separate room—while allowing the defendant to see and cross-examine the witness via video cameras—was perfectly acceptable.

The Compulsory Process Clause

Compulsory process gives the defendant the right to use subpoenas to bring witnesses to testify during the trial, just as the prosecution does. A subpoena is a court order commanding a person to appear in court. Compulsory process may be used to call anyone to testify or to produce certain documents, if the defendant can show that the witness or evidence is relevant to the case.

During the court case United States v. Nixon, the Supreme Court called President Richard M. Nixon as a compulsory witness. Courtesy of the Library of Congress.

LIMITS TO THE COMPULSORY PROCESS. If a trial judge believes a defendant's request for a witness is petty or unnecessary, the court may refuse to call the witness. Also, if the defense subpoenas a witness and the court makes a legitimate effort to bring the witness to court with no results, the Supreme Court has ruled that the accused's rights are not violated by the absence of that witness.

Furthermore, the Fifth Amendment right to refuse to testify against oneself (see "The Self-incrimination Clause" section in chapter five) is not overruled by compulsory process; therefore, a defendant cannot force witnesses to testify against themselves.

Sixth Amendment

THE HIGH, THE MIGHTY, AND THE HYPNOTIZED. Despite such limits, compulsory process can be used to call almost anyone to testify or provide evidence, if the evidence is relevant to the case. In *United States v. Nixon* (1974), for instance, the Supreme Court ruled that President Richard M. Nixon's executive privilege (presidential rights) were overruled by compulsory process.

During a trial involving some of the president's staff members and political supporters, the prosecutor subpoenaed certain tapes and documents from the president. President Nixon (1913–1994) moved to stop the subpoena. But the Court ruled that the president must produce the evidence, saying that the "constitutional need" for all relevant evidence in a case to be weighted made it necessary that "compulsory process be available for the production of evidence needed either by the prosecution or by the defense."

In a 1987 case, *Rock v. Arkansas,* the Supreme Court determined that the Compulsory Process Clause also guaranteed a defendant's right to testify on his or her own behalf. In the case the defendant had been charged with shooting her husband. After undergoing hypnosis, the defendant remembered details that indicated the gun had misfired.

An Arkansas law prohibited such "hypnotically refreshed" testimony from being used in court on the grounds that such testimony would be unreliable. But the Supreme Court ruled that the law violated the defendants' Sixth Amendment right to call witnesses, in this case from calling herself. The Court ruled that it was up to the prosecution to prove whether the "hypnotically refreshed" testimony was unreliable.

As a result of this case, the Sixth Amendment is understood to guarantee a defendant the right to testify in his or her own trial. (The Fifth Amendment's Self-incrimination Clause, on the other hand, allows defendants to *refuse* to testify in their own trials.)

The Right to the Assistance of Counsel

The right to the assistance of counsel means that a defendant has a right to effective legal assistance from someone well-versed in the law, such as a lawyer. The right to counsel far surpasses any other constitutional right of the accused. While the right to counsel was originally understood simply to mean that a defendant had the right to hire a lawyer, the Supreme Court has expanded the right to counsel considerably.

Providing lawyers for indigent defendants

In *Powell v. Alabama* (1932) Powell was one of nine young black defendants charged with raping two white women on a train that was going through Scottsboro, Alabama. The defendants could not read, had no friends or relatives in the area, and were faced with such negative publicity that the militia was called in to maintain public order.

On the morning of the trial, the judge appointed two local lawyers who reluctantly represented the multiple defendants, despite having no time to prepare their case. Trials for each defendant took just one day, and all the defendants were convicted and sentenced to death.

The Supreme Court overturned the convictions in the "Scottsboro trial," ruling that the assistance of counsel is a "fundamental" part of a defendant's right to a fair trial. The Court took the defendant's illiteracy into account as well, ruling that in this case the defendants could not have defended themselves.

The Court also said that states must provide assistance of counsel to all indigent defendants (defendants who cannot afford to hire counsel) charged with a capital crime. Furthermore, the Court ruled that the right to counsel necessarily means "effective" counsel: that is, lawyers who actually help the defendant. The ruling was also used to ensure that illiterate or "feeble-minded" defendants also should be provided with attorneys, since they could not effectively defend themselves.

In *Johnson v. Zerbst* (1938) the Court extended the *Powell* ruling to guarantee a defendant's right to receive counsel in *all* federal criminal cases. And in the historic 1963 case of *Gideon v. Wainwright* the Supreme Court used the Fourteenth Amendment (see chapter fourteen) to extend the assistance of counsel to all felony cases at the state level as well. In that case, the Court ruled that it was the government's duty to provide a lawyer to any defendant who could not otherwise afford one. (see "Gideon v. Wainwright" box.)

The right to effective counsel

As noted in *Powell v. Alabama,* the mere presence of a lawyer does not ensure a defendant's right to assistance of counsel. The assistance must also be effective—that is, the lawyer must actually help the defendant.

Deciding when a lawyer is effective is difficult, since there are many levels of effectiveness. In *Strickland v. Washington* (1984) the Supreme Court adopted the "objective reasonably competent" standard to determine whether a lawyer had provided "effective" counsel. Under this

GIDEON V. WAINWRIGHT

In 1961 Clarence Gideon was arrested in Panama City, Florida. Fifty-year old Gideon was charged with breaking into the Bay Harbor Poolroom with the intent to commit burglary. He had only an eighth-grade education and was also quite poor. While waiting for his trial Gideon researched the law and became convinced that the Sixth Amendment right to have "the assistance of counsel" combined with the Fourteenth Amendment's "due process" clause (see chapter fourteen) guaranteed him the right to a court-appointed attorney.

Florida law only required the state to provide an attorney to poor defendants in capital cases. (Capital cases involve a state's most serious crimes, such as murder or rape.) Gideon was not given a lawyer and was convicted of breaking into the poolroom.

From prison, Gideon argued that he was wrongly imprisoned by the Florida Department of Corrections, since he had not had assistance of counsel at his trial. Gideon, who still had no legal presentation, petitioned the Supreme Court of the United States to consider his case. Upon receiving the petition, written in pencil on prison paper, the Court appointed attorney Abe Fortas to argue Gideon's case.

In *Gideon v. Wainwright* (Wainwright, the director of Florida's Department of Corrections, was named as the defendant in the case), Fortas argued that "no man, no matter how intelligent" can effectively

standard, if a convicted defendant can prove that his or her lawyer made errors so serious that the defendant was deprived of a fair trial, the conviction can be thrown out. However, smaller errors by a lawyer do not automatically give the defendant the right to another trial.

Some mistakes by attorneys that have led to new trials for the defendant include the lawyer's failure to effectively question a witness, the failure to object to (argue against) inadmissible evidence, and the failure to raise certain defenses, such as self-defense.

Leveling the Field

Like the other Bill of Rights Amendments, the Sixth Amendment was created to limit the power of government. The government can charge

defend himself. He pointed out that even experienced lawyers typically hire attorneys to defend them in criminal cases. How then could normal defendants be expected to defend themselves in a trial?

Fortas then argued that the Fourteenth Amendment's guarantee of equal protection under the law meant that every defendant, no matter how poor, should have the same right to assistance of counsel that wealthy defendants had. The Court agreed, ruling that "any person [brought] into court, who is too poor to hire a lawyer, cannot be assured a fair trial unless counsel is provided for him." The Court added that the fact that the government hires lawyers to prosecute and that defendants with enough money hire lawyers to defend themselves was proof that having a lawyer in a criminal trial is considered a necessity, not a luxury.

The Supreme Court's decision did not only affect future cases. The decision was also deemed retroactive; that is, it applied to cases that had already been tried. In the following years, thousands of cases were reopened, and prisoners who had been convicted without the aid of a lawyer were released or given new trials.

Gideon himself was found not guilty of the original charges against him in a later trial. As he put it, the only difference between his first and second trials was that in the second "I had an attorney." Thanks to Gideon's determined efforts to have his case heard, defendants of all economic backgrounds can now say the same thing.

a defendant, but it must inform the defendant of the charges and try the defendant in a timely fashion in a public trial. The government may use professional prosecutors to argue its side of the case, but defendants may also have legal counsel. The government can call witnesses to testify, but compulsory process gives defendants the right to call their own witnesses. And while the government assists in the selection of a jury, the Sixth Amendment requires the government to take steps to ensure that jurors are not biased against the defendant before the case begins.

Taken together, the various clauses of the Sixth Amendment serve as a counterbalance to government power, helping to ensure that trials by jury—like those fought in medieval "trials by battle"—take place on a level playing field.

For More Information

Books

Abramson, Jeffrey. *We the Jury: The Jury System and the Ideal of Democracy.* New York: HarperCollins, 1994.

Adler, Stephen J. *The Jury: Trial and Error in the American Courtroom.* New York: Times Books, 1994.

Carter, Dan T. *Scottsboro: A Tragedy of the American South.* Baton Rouge, LA: Louisiana State University Press, 1979.

Dudley, Mark E. *Gideon v. Wainwright (1963): Right to Counsel.* New York: Twenty- First Century Books, 1995.

Geller, Laurence H., and Peter Hemenway. *Last Chance for Justice: The Juror's Lonely Quest.* Dallas: NCDS Press, 1997.

Hans, Valerie P., and Neil Vidmar. *Judging the Jury.* New York: Plenum Press, 1986.

Levine, James P. *Juries and Politics.* Pacific Grove, CA: Brooks/Cole Publishing Co., 1992.

Melusky, Joseph A., and Whitman H. Ridgeway. *The Bill of Rights: Our Written Legacy.* Malabar, FL: Krieger Publishing Company, 1993.

Sherrow, Victoria. *Gideon v. Wainwright: Free Legal Counsel.* Springfield, NJ: Enslow Publishers, 1995.

Wishman, Seymour. *Anatomy of a Jury: The System on Trial.* New York: Times Books, 1986.

Sources

Books

Cogan, Neil H., ed. *The Complete Bill of Rights: The Drafts, Debates, Sources, and Origins.* New York: Oxford University Press, 1997.

Cook, Joseph G. *Constitutional Rights of the Accused.* 3rd ed. St. Paul, MN.: West Group, 1996.

Encyclopedia of World Biography. Detroit: Gale Research, 1998.

Garcia, Alfredo. *The Sixth Amendment in Modern American Jurisprudence.* New York: Greenwood Press, 1992.

Heller, Francis H. *The Sixth Amendment to the Constitution of the United States: A Study in Constitutional Development.* New York: Greenwood Press, 1951.

Kurland, Philip B., and Ralph Lerner, eds. *The Founders' Constitution.* Chicago: University of Chicago Press, 1987.

Rutland, Robert Allen. *The Birth of the Bill of Rights: 1776–1791.* Rev. ed. Boston: Northeastern University Press, 1991.

West's Encyclopedia of American Law. St. Paul, MN.: West Group, 1997.

Witt, Elder. *The Supreme Court and Individual Rights.* 2nd ed. Washington, D.C.: Congressional Quarterly, 1988.

Sixth
Amendment

Seventh Amendment

In Suits at common law, where the value in controversy shall exceed twenty dollars, the right of trial by jury shall be preserved, and no fact tried by a jury, shall be otherwise reexamined in any Court of the United States, than according to the rules of the common law.

The Seventh Amendment deals with the use of juries in settling civil disputes. In a criminal case, the government seeks to *punish* a person who has broken a law. Article III of the Constitution and the Fifth Amendment both guarantee the right to a jury in criminal trials (see Introduction and chapter five).

Civil trials, on the other hand, compensate (award payment to) a person who has been physically or financially hurt by another person. The party bringing suit (legal action) is known as the plaintiff. If the plaintiff can show that the defendant caused the injury, he or she can ask the court to force the defendant to pay money or perform certain actions. This request for payment or action is known as a claim.

Not all trials involve a jury. The outcome of some trials is determined by the judge presiding over the case. However, the Seventh Amendment states that federal civil cases (those heard in federal courts) involving claims of more than twenty dollars are to be tried by a jury.

The second clause (section) of the amendment states that no fact decided by a jury can be changed by another court. This was intended to keep judges from overruling a jury's decision.

Origins of the Seventh Amendment

Since English settlers first came to America, juries have been an important part of American legal tradition. A jury is a panel of citizens brought

RATIFICATION FACTS

PROPOSED: Submitted by Congress to the states on September 25, 1789, along with the other nine amendments that comprise the Bill of Rights.

RATIFICATION: Ratified by the required three-fourths of states (eleven of fourteen): December 15, 1791. Declared to be part of the Constitution on December 15, 1791.

RATIFYING STATES: New Jersey, November 20, 1789; Maryland, December 19, 1789; North Carolina, December 22, 1789; South Carolina, January 19, 1790; New Hampshire, January 25, 1790; Delaware, January 28, 1790; New York, February 24, 1790; Pennsylvania, March 10, 1790; Rhode Island, June 7, 1790; Vermont, November 3, 1791; Virginia, December 15, 1791 (amendment adopted).

together to hear evidence, and then decide the facts, that is, what happened, in a legal case. Because juries allow ordinary citizens to play an important role in the legal system, they have long been viewed as a valuable protection against the abuse of government power.

When the British government limited colonists' right to a jury trial, the colonists protested angrily. During the American Revolution (1775–81), the colonies won their independence from Great Britain. Colonists repeatedly listed the right to a trial by jury among the basic rights they were fighting for.

After the war, the states nearly rejected the proposed Constitution of the United States, partly because it failed to guarantee the right to a jury in civil trials. The states only ratified the Constitution it was agreed a Bill of Rights would be attached.

The Seventh Amendment was part of the Bill of Rights that became part of the Constitution in 1791. The amendment guaranteed the right to a jury trial in most civil lawsuits in federal court.

A history of limitations

Despite their importance, the Supreme Court has repeatedly limited the Seventh Amendment's reach in civil jury trials over the years,. In

**Seventh
Amendment**

fact, the Court has ruled that the amendment doesn't apply to a number of types of civil suits, including:

- **Cases against the government.** A person suing the government is not entitled to a trial by jury unless Congress specifically passes a law requiring such a trial.
- **"Public rights" cases.** Cases involving new rights created by Congress (public rights) may be decided in special courts, and without a jury.
- **Maritime cases.** Cases involving navigation or commerce at sea are traditionally heard in separate courts, and decided by judges, not juries.
- **Equitable cases.** If a plaintiff seeks a court order to force a person to perform certain actions (or to stop performing others) it is known as an equitable claim. The Supreme Court has ruled that since such cases do not involve money, they are not covered by the Seventh Amendment, and may be decided without a jury.

English Roots of the American Jury

Many of the legal practices in Britain's American colonies came directly from English common law (legal tradition). Juries, in one form or another, existed in England before the first British colonists came to America at the beginning of the seventeenth century. Even then, however, juries were a relatively new feature of English law.

"Trial by ordeal"

Superstition and fate played a large role in deciding criminal trials in England before the twelfth century. One method of settling a criminal case at that time was the "trial by ordeal." In those trials, defendants (people accused of a crime) were forced to undergo potentially life-ending ordeals to decide their fates. Such ordeals included walking across red-hot metal, or being thrown in a river with hands and feet bound up. The fear of bodily harm sometimes led defendants to confess before the torture began (whether they were actually guilty or not). If a person did chose to undergo the ordeal, it was thought that God would injure the guilty, and protect the innocent.

"Trial by battle"

Another form of trial that relied on supernatural intervention was "trial by battle." Civil disputes were settled by armed combat between the opposing sides in a case. Whichever party won the fight was believed to have been favored by God, and was declared the winner of the dispute.

William I introduces changes

In 1066, William, Duke of Normandy (c. 1027–1087), invaded England and defeated King Harold. William I's new government introduced England to many elements of French Norman culture. In the years after the Norman Conquest, a new kind of trial took shape in England. Groups of people not involved in a civil dispute were asked to decide the outcome of the case. These early juries consisted of twelve men from the community who already had knowledge of the case.

These jurors, or "oath helpers" as they were called, were not quite like modern jurors. Today a juror is expected not to know the facts of a case until the trial begins. The early jurors were more like witnesses. They told the court what they already knew about the dispute. Nonetheless, these early juries were an important step away from the questionable case deciding methods that had been used before.

Jury trials quickly became popular in England. By the late 1100s, a defendant in royal court was entitled to request a jury trial, and "put himself upon his country." In 1215, the Magna Carta (an agreement between England's wealthy landowners and King John (1167–1216) specifically stated that "judgment by one's peers (equals) " should decide questions of law. By 1219, the trial by ordeal was completely abolished in England.

Jury trials become a right

In the fourteenth century, the role of juries changed fundamentally. Jurors no longer functioned as witnesses. Instead, they heard evidence that was presented *to* them. As juries became known as impartial bodies that decided what the facts were in a case, public confidence in the jury system grew. In 1689, the English Bill of Rights made the jury trial a right. The right to trial by jury was held dearly by the English people. The great English commentator and lawyer Sir William Blackstone wrote in the 1760s that the civil jury trial was "the glory of the English law."

Juries in Colonial America

From the beginning, England's colonies took steps to ensure the right to trial by jury in civil cases. Most of the original thirteen colonies established the right as part of their charters (their original body of laws).

Seventh Amendment

Also, all thirteen colonies relied on twelve-member juries to decide facts in civil cases.

Trial by jury was particularly important in the colonies. It allowed colonists to decide the outcome of their cases, rather than relying on judges paid by the far off British government. Although the royal judges who presided over the jury trials were appointed by the British government, the judges and the juries came from local communities.

Britain tightens its grip

By the middle of the 1700s, tension had grown between Great Britain and the American colonies. The British government sought new ways to raise funds, and to save money in the colonies (see chapter three). Many of the tactics the British tried angered colonists, and sparked public protests. For instance, the British government's policy of quartering (housing) soldiers in public buildings and private homes led to protests and even rioting (see chapter three). So as did attempts to impose duties (fees) and taxes on goods the colonists imported.

As American protests grew, the British began to exercise more control over the colonies. They stationed more soldiers in "trouble spots," such as Boston. (During the Boston Tea Party (1773) protesters had dumped tons of English tea into the bay rather than pay a duty on it.)

The British also took steps to keep local juries from finding in favor of protesters charged with crimes. The government took away the absolute right to trial by jury. And for some crimes, colonists were shipped off to England without any guarantee of a fast or fair trial (see chapter six).

British authorities also reorganized the civil courts. Admiralty courts traditionally had the power to deal with maritime law (legal matters involving ships at sea). These cases were decided by a single judge rather than by a jury. Beginning in the 1760s, the British transferred control of many civil cases to these maritime courts. This meant that judges appointed by the British government now decided cases that juries had previously heard before.

Juries and revolution

THE DECLARATION OF RIGHTS. The maritime courts were very effective in limiting the control that colonists had over the legal process. The changes also increased the colonist's resentment of British rule. The 1774

Declaration of Rights outlined the rights the colonies felt they were entitled to from the British government. One of the central rights the colonies insisted on was the right to trial by jury. "The respective colonies are entitled to the common law of England," the document read. "[A]nd more especially to the great and inestimable privilege of being tried by their peers of the vicinage [area], according to course of that law."

Notice that the colonists claimed that the right was promised by the "common law of England." It's interesting that it was the colonists desire to be treated like English citizens that led to the break between England and America.

THE DECLARATION OF INDEPENDENCE. The Declaration of Rights did little to change relations between Great Britain and the colonies. In 1775, war broke out between American soldiers and the British Army. On July 4, 1776, after more than a year of fighting, the colonies drafted a formal Declaration of Independence, declaring the colonies separation from Great Britain. Among the reasons the Declaration of Independence listed for the split with Great Britain was the fact that the British government had deprived colonists "in many cases, of the benefits of Trial by Jury."

Restoring the Civil Jury

After the colonies declared their independence, all thirteen of the former colonies, now states, restored the right to trial by jury. Ten states specifically mentioned the right to a civil jury trial in their constitutions. The other three—Delaware, South Carolina, and Connecticut —either passed laws, or simply implemented juries in common practice.

The importance the right held for the states is seen in the language they used to establish it. New York ensured that trial by jury "shall be established and remain inviolate (unbroken) forever." New Jersey's constitution also guaranteed that the right would stand "forever." Massachusetts and New Hampshire's constitutions declared that the right "shall be held sacred."

Juries, the new Constitution, and a Bill of Rights

Even as the states established their own constitutions, the larger question of how to form a single nation from the various states was still unanswered. In 1781, the states formed a loose union under the Articles of Confederation. However, the government formed by the Articles had very little power.

Seventh Amendment

The civil jury insures fair court rulings at yet another, lower, level of the government court system. Reproduced by permission of AP/ Wide World Photos.

By 1786, many people called for the formation of a stronger national government. During the Constitutional Convention held in Philadelphia, Pennsylvania, from May 23 to September 17, 1787, representatives from twelve of the states met to design a constitution for a new federal government.

Surprisingly, though the civil jury had been extremely important at the state level, the representatives to the convention did not include any mention of the right in the proposed U.S. Constitution. In fact, the new Constitution lacked any list of individual rights. Public outcry over this oversight led to an agreement between backers of the new Constitution (the Federalists) and those who opposed it (Anti-Federalists). It was agreed that a Bill of Rights would be added as soon as the states ratified the Constitution.

The right to civil jury trials was especially important to citizens who feared the power the new national government would have over them. Six of the states that ratified the new Constitution specifically called for an amendment ensuring civil jury trials.

James Madison (1751–1836), a Virginia lawyer who later became the fourth president of the United States, wrote the first draft of the Bill

of Rights in 1789. His first draft of the Seventh Amendment read: "In suits at common law, between man and man, the trial by jury, as one of the best securities to the rights of the people, ought to remain inviolate (unbreakable)." Over the next three months, Congress (the lawmaking body of the federal government) changed the amendment's wording. The revised version read: "In suits at common law, where the value in controversy shall exceed twenty dollars, the right of trial by jury shall be preserved, and no fact tried by a jury, shall be otherwise reexamined in any Court of the United States, than according to the rules of the common law."

In addition to guaranteeing jury trials in cases where claims exceeded twenty dollars, the new amendment also limited a judge's power to overrule (change) a jury's decision. The Seventh Amendment was ratified with the rest of the Bill of Rights amendments on December 15, 1791. Virginia was the eleventh and final state (of the fourteen states then in existence) to ratify the amendments (see Introduction).

The Courts Interpret the Law

Under the U.S. Constitution, the Supreme Court of the United States is the highest court in the nation. The Court has the final power to decide how courts and other government bodies interpret laws. However, since the Supreme Court can overrule (change) its own decisions, interpretation of a particular law may change over time.

Deciding which cases are entitled to juries

The Seventh Amendment is stated in a fairly straightforward manner, and at first glance wouldn't seem to require much interpretation. In civil cases involving more than twenty dollars, the right of "trial by jury shall be preserved" and "no fact (decided) by a jury, shall be otherwise reexamined in any Court of the United States" except "according to the rules of the common law." This last phrase—"according to the rules of the common law"—however, raises some important questions: What are "the rules of common law," and can they limit the right to a jury?

In 1812, a federal circuit court (a lower court that hears cases from a particular region of the United States) issued the first interpretation of the Seventh Amendment. Although the case was not heard by the Supreme Court, the decision in the case of *United States v. Wonson* had a lasting impact on the way the Seventh Amendment was understood.

Seventh Amendment

The federal government had lost a lawsuit against Samuel Wonson in a jury trial. The government argued that it had the right to retry the facts with a second jury trial in the New England Circuit Court. The government said that since certain states in New England allowed a retrial by a second jury, the "common law" of New England dictated that the circuit court for that region should allow retrial as well.

District court judge Joseph Story (1779–1845) rejected this argument. After examining the history of the Seventh Amendment, Story said that the "obvious intention" of the clause was to prevent a higher court from retrying or overruling a jury's decisions. Story also ruled that the phrase "common law" in the Seventh Amendment did not refer to the statutes and legal history of the states. Story wrote that "[b]eyond all question, the common law here alluded (referred) to is ... the common law of England, the grand reservoir of all our jurisprudence (legal tradition)."

After *Wonson,* courts would determine whether to order a civil jury trial by referring to English common law. Under this "historical test," if a court determined that a party in a civil case would have been entitled to a jury trial under English common law, then he or she was entitled to one in the United States, too.

The "fixed historical test"

During the nineteenth century, English courts limited the use of civil jury trials. They reserved juries for special types of civil cases. The United States did not follow these changes in English law. In *Thompson v. Utah* (1891), the Supreme Court ruled that the historical test courts used to determine whether a case deserved a jury trial must use English common law as it was in 1791, the year the Bill of Rights went into effect. The court ruled that the meaning of the terms "jury" and "trial by jury" were attached to the English common law at a *fixed* time. These terms should always keep "the law as it was in this country and in England at the time" the Bill of Rights were adopted. Though *Thompson* was a criminal case, the Supreme Court later adopted this "fixed historical test" for establishing civil jury rights.

Not All Cases are Created Equal

Whether a litigant (party in a lawsuit) is entitled to a jury trial depends on the type of claim involved. Claims against the government are always treated differently than other civil actions. But even cases involving two private (non-government) parties are not always entitled to a jury.

CIVIL CASES IN STATE COURTS

State governments are not required by the Constitution or the Seventh Amendment to provide jury trials in civil cases. The Bill of Rights was drafted in 1789 to limit the powers of the federal government, not the state governments. However, the Fourteenth Amendment (ratified by the states in 1868; see chapter fourteen) included a clause, or section, that has since been used to apply the Bill of Rights to the actions of the state governments.

The Fourteenth Amendment's Due Process Clause forbids states from depriving any person of life, liberty, or property without due process of law. Beginning with *Gitlow v. New York* (1925), the Supreme Court used this clause to apply many of the Bill of Rights amendments to the state governments. In *Gitlow,* the Court found that state governments must protect the First Amendment's freedom of speech, assembly and worship (see chapter one).

The Supreme Court, however, has never applied the Seventh Amendment to the states. In 1916, the Court refused to require states to provide a civil jury trial in the case of *Minneapolis & St. Louis Railroad v. Bombolis.* And in *Hardware Dealers' Mut. Fire Ins. Co. of Wisconsin v. Glidden Co.* (1931), the Court declared that the Fourteenth Amendment "neither implies that all trials must be by jury, nor guarantees any particular form or method of state procedure."

Despite the fact that the Supreme Court hasn't applied the Seventh Amendment to state governments, civil jury trials exist in most states. Just as it was at the time of the American Revolution, most state constitutions contain guarantees very similar to those found in the Seventh Amendment.

Maritime law

Maritime cases have traditionally been treated differently than other civil cases, even in Colonial times. In *Parsons v. Bedford* (1830), the Supreme Court used the historical test to determine that cases involving maritime law do not guarantee a jury trial, since they had never been heard by juries under English common law.

Equitable cases

When a plaintiff seeks money it is called a *legal* claim. However, a plaintiff may also ask a court to order the defendant to perform certain actions, or to stop performing others. Such requests are known as *equitable* claims. It is often difficult to categorize a claim as legal or equitable. Since equitable claims do not involve money, the Supreme Court has ruled that they are not covered by the Seventh Amendment, and may be decided without a jury.

However, the distinction between legal and equitable claims is sometimes hard to determine, even for courts. Lawsuits asking for restitution (making good for loss or damage) have been treated as both legal and equitable cases, depending on the court.

Patent cases

Patent cases deal with the ownership of new inventions. In *Markman v. Westview Instruments, Inc.* (1996), the Supreme Court ruled that many questions raised in a patent case are questions of law. A question of law deals with how the law applies to the particular facts of a case. Juries tra-

Maritime cases are not always entitled to a jury. Reproduced by permission of Susan D. Rock.

ditionally only settle questions of fact—that is, they decide what happened in a particular case. A judge decides questions of law: do the facts in the case entitle the plaintiff to compensation? In *Markman,* the Court found that many patent cases do not involve questions of fact, only questions of law. Such cases, the Court ruled, may be tried without a jury.

Suing Uncle Sam

Under English common law, the sovereign (the king or queen, or more generally the government) could do no wrong, and was therefore immune (protected) from civil lawsuits. But, under certain circumstances, the king would permit a party to sue his government. His consent was usually required before such a lawsuit could go forward.

When the federal government of the United States faced lawsuits, the ancient concept of sovereign immunity was revived. The Supreme Court invoked the concept in the early cases of *Chisholm v. Georgia* (1793) and *Cohens v. Virginia* (1821). In these cases, the Court held that the federal government was immune from lawsuits unless Congress authorized them. Through the mid-nineteenth century, people who felt that they had been injured by the federal government had to ask Congress, on a case-by-case basis, to pass a special bill that would compensate them for their injuries.

The Court of Claims

In 1855 Congress established the U.S. Court of Claims. This was the first court in which plaintiffs could directly sue the federal government. In the Court of Claims, a judge, not a jury, ruled on all the facts in a case.

Over the next one hundred years, Congress established other courts for people to bring various suits against the government. However, in almost every case where suits against the government were allowed, Congress dictated that there was no right to a trial by jury. In *McElrath v. United States* (1880), the Supreme Court ruled that such actions were perfectly legal. Thomas L. McElrath was a former Navy lieutenant. He sued the government for back pay, and the case was heard by a judge in the Court of Claims. The judge ruled in favor of the government. McElrath argued that his Seventh Amendment rights had been violated since no jury had heard his case. The Supreme Court rejected this argument, using the concept of sovereign immunity to justify its decision.

The Court reasoned that since people can only sue the government when it allows itself to be sued, the government has the freedom to determine how it will be sued. Therefore, it has the right to decide whether cases against it will be heard by a jury or not. In other words, the Supreme Court said that suits against the government "are not controlled by the Seventh Amendment."

Directed verdicts

In the case of *Galloway v. United States* (1943), the court ruled that even when a jury hears a case, a judge still may overrule (set aside) the verdict. Freda Galloway sued the government over benefits she claimed were owed to her husband, a veteran of World War I. The case was heard in a federal district court. The judge ruled against Galloway in a *directed verdict*. (A directed verdict is one in which the judge, without any input from the jury, throws a case out due to a lack of evidence.)

Galloway appealed the decision to the Supreme Court. She argued that the directed verdict violated her guarantee to a jury trial under the Seventh Amendment. In this case, the Court used the concepts of sovereign immunity, and the "fixed historical test" to deny Galloway's claim. The Court said no one could argue "that under the common law in 1791 jury trial was a matter of right for persons [suing] the sovereign."

Government must specify jury trial

In *Lehman v. Nakshian* (1981), the Court ruled that even when Congress doesn't prohibit a jury trial, a plaintiff with a case against the government does not have the absolute right for a jury trial. Under the Age Discrimination in Employment Act of 1967 (ADEA), private and *government* employers are forbidden from discriminating against workers over the age of forty. The law waives the government's sovereign immunity in such cases, and allows government employees to sue the government for age discrimination. However, the law made no mention of whether juries should hear these cases.

When Alice Nakshian sued the Navy for age discrimination, she argued that the Seventh Amendment guaranteed her a jury trial. But the Supreme Court ruled that in cases against the government, the right to a jury trial only exists if Congress specifically grants it. Since the ADEA did not mention juries one way or the other, the Court ruled that Nakshian was not entitled to a jury trial.

Congressional restrictions and sovereign immunity

Almost every time Congress waived the government's sovereign immunity, it has required parties who sue the government to give up "any claim to a jury trial." For instance, in the Claims Act of 1946, Congress passed a bill that allowed citizens to sue the government in the existing district courts, but *without a jury.*

Even when Congress did allow jury trials against the government, it limited the jury's power. A 1957 bill allowed for jury trials in certain tax refund cases. But Congress was concerned that juries "might tend to be overly generous," and limited the amount of money a jury could award a plaintiff.

Thus, the concept of sovereign immunity has allowed Congress to routinely prevent juries from hearing cases against the government. And the Supreme Court has ruled that the Seventh Amendment simply does not apply to claims against the government.

Public Rights

The idea that civil suits against the government are not covered by the Seventh Amendment guarantee to a jury trial is known as the *public rights exception.* As the federal government grew in size and in power during the twentieth century, this exception was used to exempt more and more cases from juries hearing them.

A new kind of court

Under the Tariff Act of 1922, Congress gave the president the authority to impose customs (taxes on imported goods), and established a Tariff Commission to determine what those customs should be. The act also created the Court of Customs and Patent Appeals, in part to settle disputes over these new taxes. In *Ex Parte Bakelite Corp.* (1929), the Supreme Court declared that the new court was a "legislative" court with both judicial and legislative power. Judicial power is the power to decide legal disputes, and legislative power is the power to create laws or rules.

The Court ruled that Congress could create new kinds of rights that were not covered by common law traditions. Furthermore, Congress had the right to decide how disputes over these new "public rights" were tried. In this case, Congress created the president's right to impose customs. Therefore, it could also decide how customs disputes were handled. Congress could allow such cases to be tried in ordinary courts, or in new courts specifically set up for that purpose.

DEFINING THE CIVIL JURY

In the late twentieth century, the courts considered several questions regarding civil juries, such as: how small could a jury be? What degree of impartiality (fairness) was required? To what extent could judges overrule the jury?

Traditionally, civil juries consisted of twelve people. This number had existed under English common law, and was used in early legal practice in the United States. But by 1973, more than fifty U.S. district courts adopted local rules that cut the size of the civil jury in half. In *Colgrove v. Battin* (1973), the Supreme Court found that these smaller juries in no way violated the Seventh Amendment. The Court held that the language of the amendment "is not directed to jury characteristics," but rather to the types of cases that are entitled to juries. The Court went on to say that the quality of a juries decision making was not weakened by having six members instead of twelve.

Federal courts have long recognized that both the Due Process Clause of the Fifth Amendment (see chapter five) and the Seventh Amendment guarantee an impartial (unbiased) jury in civil trials. A party's right to an impartial jury is presumed violated whenever a juror communicates without permission to anyone outside of the courtroom—including friends, relatives, or journalists.

If such communication takes place, it is up to one of the parties in the case to prove that the communication did not lead to a tainted jury.

Congress could even establish special boards or agencies to settle disputes without a trial. And because common law did not apply to these public rights (since the rights did not exist before 1791), the Seventh Amendment did not apply to them, and Congress was not required to provide for jury trials.

Public rights versus private rights

In *Crowell v. Benson,* a worker sued his non-government employer for compensation. Under common law, such cases between two private parties were decided by trial juries. However, Congress had previously set up the U.S. Employees Compensation Commission to settle such disputes, without juries.

(A jury is considered tainted or compromised when one or more of its members no longer can decide the facts fairly or honestly.) The presence of even one biased juror can violate a party's Seventh Amendment rights. In *Haley v. Blue Ridge Transfer Co.* (1986), the Fourth Circuit Court of Appeals overturned a verdict because a non-juror was accidentally seated with the jury for one day before the trial began.

Judges and juries have separate powers in a civil jury trial. Judges instruct juries on the law; jurors listen to the evidence, determine which facts are relevant, and reach a verdict or decision. The second clause of the Seventh Amendment prohibits federal judges from reexamining the facts in a case after juries have tried them. A jury's verdict cannot be overturned as long as it is *reasonably* supported by the evidence.

Furthermore, a jury must be allowed to hear a lawsuit in its entirety, from start to finish. In *Gregory v. Missouri Pacific Railroad* (1994), the Fifth Circuit Court of Appeals ordered a new trial in an injury case, because the jury had not been allowed to hear a relevant piece of testimony.

However, there are times when a judge makes the final decision in a case. Judges may overrule a jury's decision if it is found unreasonable—that is, if the judge finds that the facts do not in any way support the jury's verdict. Also, if a judge determines that a plaintiff simply does not have enough evidence to support the claim, the judge may issue a "directed verdict." If this happens, the case is thrown out without consulting the jury, or without allowing it to hear the entire case.

The Supreme Court said that while the dispute involved a private right, Congress had replaced the traditional common law approach with a new federal compensation scheme. Therefore, Congress decided how compensation disputes were settled. The ruling suggested that Congress had the power to create new, jury-less forums for resolving disputes.

In 1970, Congress created the Occupational Safety and Health Review Commission (OSHRC) to rule in cases involving workplace safety complaints. If the commission found that an employer had broken federal safety laws, the employer could appeal the OSHRC decision in federal court. However, a judge would decide the appeal, not a jury.

In *Atlas Roofing Co. v. Occupational Safety & Health Review Commission* (1977), Atlas Roofing argued that the lack of a jury trial vio-

Seventh Amendment

lated the Seventh Amendment. The Supreme Court rejected Atlas's claim on the grounds that Congress's authority over public rights extended to new areas. Federal lawmakers could create new statutory public rights (such as the right to a safe workplace), and assign cases concerning those rights to an agency (rather than a court) without violating the Seventh Amendment. The Court said that traditional common law rights could not be written into new statutes and then transferred out of normal courts. It also ruled that a government agency, rather than a court, could only decide cases in which the government was a party.

A Disappearing Act or Expanding Rights?

Critics of the Supreme Court argue that an American's right to a civil jury trial has slowly been stripped away, as the Court rules that more and more types of lawsuits are not covered by the Seventh Amendment. Indeed, the number of cases heard without a jury has grown dramatically since 1791.

In most cases, the Seventh Amendment was found not to apply under the concept of sovereign immunity. These are cases against the government, which even in early American history, the government could have simply refused to allow.

In fact, since the mid-1800s, a citizen's power to sue the government has consistently expanded. It's true that Congress has seldom allowed for jury trials in such cases. But beginning with the establishment of the U.S. Court of Claims in 1855, Congress has made it easier to sue the government —in cases involving traditional rights as well as in a whole new class of public rights cases.

Sources

Books

Hall, Kermit L., ed. *Oxford Companion to the Supreme Court of the United States.* New York: Oxford University Press, 1992.

West's Encyclopedia of American Law. St. Paul, MN: West Group, 1998.

Articles

Carrington, Paul D. "The Seventh Amendment: Some Bicentennial Reflections." *University of Chicago Legal Forum* (1990): 33.

Grant, Eric. "A Revolutionary View of the Seventh Amendment and the Just Compensation Clause." *Northwestern University Law Review* Number 91 (Fall 1996): 144.

Klein, Kenneth S. "The Myth of How to Interpret the Seventh Amendment Right to a Civil Jury Trial." *Ohio State Law Journal* Number 53 (1992): 1005.

"The Validity of the Public Rights Doctrine in Light of the Historical Rationale of the Seventh Amendment." *Hastings Constitutional Law Quarterly* Number 21 (Spring 1994): 1013.

Murphy, Collen P. "Determining Compensation: The Tension Between Legislative Power and Jury Authority." *Texas Law Review* Number 74 (December 1995): 345.

Schwartz, Rachael E. "'Everything Depends on How You Draw the Lines': An Alternative Interpretation of the Seventh Amendment." *Seton Hall Constitutional Law Journal* Number 6 (Spring 1996): 599.

Weeden, Jason. "Historically Immune Defendants and the Seventh Amendment." *Texas Law Review* Number 74 (February 1996): 655.

Wolfram, Charles W. "The Constitutional History of the Seventh Amendment." *Minnesota Law Review* Number 57 (1973): 639.

Young, Gordon G. "Public Rights and the Federal Judicial Power: From Murray's Lessee through Crowell to Schor." *Buffalo Law Review* Number 35 (Fall 1986): 765.

Eighth Amendment

Excessive bail shall not be required, nor excessive fines imposed, nor cruel and unusual punishments inflicted.

The Eighth Amendment was put in place to prevent the government from unfairly punishing defendants and criminals before and after trial. Punishment is any action taken against a person who has committed an offense. Most legal punishments are created by legislatures (the law-making branch of government), and then imposed, or handed out, by courts. Punishments include:

- **Fines:** a fine is a sum of money one party is required to pay to another party as punishment for an offense.

- **Corporal (bodily) punishment:** this form of punishment has largely been phased out of the American legal system. But at one time whipping, branding, and even the slicing off of a criminal's ear or finger were common punishments.

- **Incarceration (imprisonment):** since the Eighth Amendment was drafted, incarceration has become a common form of punishment. Criminals are now sentenced to time behind bars for a wide variety of crimes, including theft and murder.

- **Capital Punishment (the death penalty):** a person convicted of a "capital crime" may be sentenced to death. The government's definition of capital crimes has changed over time. Today murder, crimes in which a person died during the commission (act) of a crime, and certain drug crimes are punishable by death in the United States.

- **Pretrial Incarceration:** defendants who are kept in jail awaiting trial are, in effect, being punished before they've been found guilty of an offense. The bail system allows defendants to pay a sum of

RATIFICATION FACTS

PROPOSED: Submitted by Congress to the states on September 25, 1789, along with the other nine amendments that comprise the Bill of Rights.

RATIFICATION: Ratified by the required three-fourths of states (eleven of fourteen) on December 15, 1791. Declared to be part of the Constitution on December 15, 1791.

RATIFYING STATES: New Jersey, November 20, 1789; Maryland, December 19, 1789; North Carolina, December 22, 1789; South Carolina, January 19, 1790; New Hampshire, January 25, 1790; Delaware, January 28, 1790; New York, February 24, 1790; Pennsylvania, March 10, 1790; Rhode Island, June 7, 1790; Vermont, November 3, 1791; Virginia, December 15, 1791 (amendment adopted).

money (bail) to the court in order to get out of jail before his or her trial. The bail serves as the defendant's promise or guarantee not to flee (run away). If the defendant fails to appear at trial, he or she forfeits (loses) the bail money, and faces additional criminal charges. Bail allows defendants to escape pretrial punishment, and makes it easier for a defendant to prepare for trial.

The following are descriptions of the three short separate clauses contained in the Eighth amendment that each deal with courts and defendants:

- The **Excessive Bail Clause:** prohibits the government from setting bail at an inappropriately high amount.

- The **Excessive Fines Clause:** bans the government from imposing "excessive" fines.

- The **Cruel and Unusual Punishments Clause:** bans the government from inflicting punishments considered "cruel and unusual." Some believe this clause limits the government from inflicting corporal or capital punishment of any kind. Others believe the clause requires the government to make sure that a punishment is proportionate to (in balance with) the crime being punished.

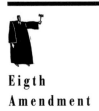

Origins of the Eight Amendment

The practice of issuing bail to criminal defendants dates as far back as seventh-century England. At that time, a person accused of a murder was required to pay a sum of money (known as bohr) to the murder victim's family. If the defendant was later found innocent of the crime, the bohr was returned.

In ninth and tenth century England, a similar system rose up to handle defendants before trial. Judges used to travel from county to county hearing local cases. A town's sheriff was responsible for holding defendants until these traveling courts came to town. But holding defendants was expensive, and Sheriffs often released defendants who posted a sum of money as a promise that they would show up at trial. However, this early bail system was subject to abuse. Sheriffs could set bail at very high amounts in order to take advantage of wealthy defendants, or to keep some defendants in jail.

The first law that imposed a legal standard for setting bail in England was the First Statute of Westminster (1275). This law required that bail be set for certain crimes, but also prohibited bail for crimes such as murder, treason, and jail-breaking.

Raising money for the King

Sheriffs weren't the only officials who took advantage of England's early legal system. Judges often imposed huge fines that were clearly out of proportion (or balance) with the actual offense being punished. Often the court's purpose in imposing such large fines was not to punish the offender, but to raise money for the Crown (the King or Queen of England). This practice became especially common during the reign of King James II (1633–1701). His rule from 1685 until 1688 helped spur the passage of the English Bill of Rights in 1689 (see below).

Putting the hurt on criminals

Bail and fines were excessive in England, but other punishments were even worse. As late as the seventeenth century, England's courts inflicted many harsh corporal punishments. Such punishments included: drawing and quartering (authorities cut off a man's arms and legs and removed his inner organs while he was still alive); branding (burning with a hot iron); whipping; and cutting off body parts (such as ears or fingers).

Early punishments were more likely to be harsh corporal punishments, such as the post and pillary. Courtesy of the Library of Congress.

In seventeenth-century England, capital punishment (punishment by death) was very common. Some 250 crimes were punishable by death under England's legal system. It's no wonder that it was nicknamed the "Bloody Code." Even as late as 1823, the theft of small amounts of money was still punishable by death.

The English Bill of Rights

In 1689, Britain's Parliament (legislature) passed the English Bill of Rights. This statute made Parliament the main political power in Great

**Eigth
Amendment**

Britain, and granted the people of Great Britain certain inviolable (unbreakable) rights. Article 10 of the English Bill of Rights stated that "excessive bail ought not to be required, nor excessive fines imposed, nor cruel and unusual punishments inflicted." These clauses were eventually used, almost word for word, by the drafters of the Eighth Amendment.

Punishment in Early America

The men and women who came to Britain's colonies (territories) in North America in the 1600s brought with them much of England's common law, or legal traditions. And though colonists elected local governments, ultimately they were still under the rule of the British government. As a result, the colonial legal system remained closely tied to the English legal system. Corporal punishment was common, as were several types of capital punishment, including death by hanging and burning at the stake.

By the middle of the 1700s, disputes (fights) over taxes, government representation, and the large number of British soldiers being stationed in America led to a split between the American colonies and Great Britain (see Introduction). The colonies eventually fought for—and won—their independence in the American Revolutionary War (1775–1783).

After the war, the former colonies (now thirteen independent states) united under the Articles of Confederation (see Introduction) to create a loose-knit nation. From May 23 to September 17, 1787 delegates from the states came together in Philadelphia to create the Constitution of the United States. The Constitution outlined a new form of government, and was divided into three branches:

- The executive branch (led by the president): responsible for carrying out the laws and policies of the new government;

- The legislative branch (Congress): responsible for making laws, raising funds, and declaring war, among other things; and

- The judicial branch (the court system, headed by the Supreme Court): responsible for interpreting all of the nation's laws.

The new Constitution was ratified (approved) by the states in 1788. However, during public debates, many citizens and politicians objected to the fact that the new Constitution did not have a Bill of Rights, or a list of individual rights. The proposed federal (national) government was

*An early form of
the death penalty
was being beheaded
at the guillotine.*
Reproduced by permission
of the Corbis Corporation
(Bellevue).

much more powerful than it had been under the Articles of Confederation. Citizens worried that the government might abuse its powers. In order to win public support for the Constitution, its supporters agreed to add a Bill of Rights as soon as Congress was in place.

In 1789, the new federal government was established, and Congress convened (met) for the first time. General George Washington (1732–1799) was the supreme commander of the colonies' forces during the American Revolutionary War. He took office as the first president of the United States. The new Congress quickly undertook the business of

**Eigth
Amendment**

drafting the amendments (or changes) to the Constitution that would eventually become America's Bill of Rights.

The language of the Eighth amendment was taken almost directly from the English Bill of Rights. (George Mason [1725–1782] from Virginia had inserted the same words into Virginia's Declaration of Rights in 1776.) Congress approved the Eighth Amendment in 1789 after very little debate.

A TASTE OF DEBATES TO COME. During the discussions over the Bill of Rights Amendments in Congress, Representative William Smith of South Carolina asked, "What is meant by the term 'excessive bail?' Who are to be the judges? What is understood by 'excessive fines?' It lays with the court to determine." Representative Smith worried that the vague terms would eventually make it hard for the government to punishment criminals at all.

A man from Virginia had a very different concern about the Eighth Amendment's wording. Patrick Henry (1736–1799) was a celebrated Revolutionary War leader. He worried that the vague wording left the government with *too much* power to set punishments for crimes. "No latitude (freedom) ought to be left [to Congress]," warned Henry. "[Y]our members of Congress will loose the restriction of not imposing excessive fines, demanding excessive bail, and inflicting cruel and unusual punishments."

Despite Henry and Smith's opposite concerns, the Eighth Amendment was ratified (agreed to) by the states on December 15, 1791 along with the other nine amendments to the Constitution that became known as America's Bill of Rights.

The Highest Court in the Land

The ultimate power to interpret the Constitution and its various amendments belongs to the Supreme Court of the United States. The Court originally consisted of six justices (judges), but was expanded to nine justices in 1869.

Justices may write individual opinions (judgments) about a case, or sign another justice's opinion. Regardless of how many opinions the Court issues, the final ruling is always decided when the judges make a simple vote. It is not uncommon for the Supreme Court to change its own interpretation of law from one case to another.

Defining Excessive Bail in the Courts

The same year the Eighth Amendment was drafted, Congress passed the Judiciary Act of 1789. The Judiciary Act established that all defendants (except those accused capital crimes) had a right to bail.

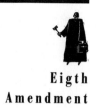
The idea that defendants accused of capital crimes aren't eligible for bail is as old as the system of bail itself. Since defendants in such cases face the death sentence, it is believed that no amount of bail can guarantee a defendant will not try to flee. As an Alabama court put it by quoting the Bible in *Ex parte McAnally* (1875), "[A]ll that a man (has), he will give for his life."

However, the Eight Amendment has a gap, because it doesn't specifically say that a defendant has the right to bail—it merely bans "excessive" bail. The Judiciary Act of 1789 filled that gap.

In cases such as *Hudson v. Parker* (1895), the Supreme Court stressed the importance of bail. The Court stated that bail provided a defendant with the opportunity to better prepare a defense, and avoid punishment before trial. But neither the Court's decisions nor the Judiciary Act of 1789 defined what exactly was meant by "excessive bail."

Way too much

In *Stack v. Boyle* (1951), the Supreme Court finally set some guidelines for setting appropriate bail. A lower court had set bail at $50,000 for each of twelve defendants charged with advocating (arguing for) the violent overthrow of the federal government. The defendants argued that the high bail violated the Excessive Bail Clause.

The government's lawyers claimed that the high bail was needed, because without it the defendants would flee. The Supreme Court agreed that the purpose of bail was to ensure that defendants showed up at trial. The Court found no evidence that showed the defendants were especially likely to avoid trial.

The Court ruled that "[b]ail set at a figure higher than an amount reasonably calculated to [keep a defendant from fleeing] is 'excessive' under the Eighth Amendment." It ordered the lower court to set bail at a reasonable amount for each defendant.

The *Stack* decision suggested that the only function of bail was to ensure defendants appeared at trial. According to *Stack,* if the government wanted to set an unusually high bail, it had to show proof that a defendant was likely to flee.

RETOOLING AMERICA'S BAIL SYSTEM

The Supreme Court is the ultimate judge of deciding whether procedures used by the government for setting bail are constitutional or not. But Congress has the power to create laws regulating how bail is set. The legislature first shaped the bail system with the Judiciary Act of 1789 when it created laws that gave defendants in non-capital cases the right to bail. In the second half of the twentieth century, Congress overhauled the country's bail system twice.

In the 1960s, studies showed that many defendants were kept in jail before trial simply because they were poor. According to these studies, defendants who could not afford to pay bail stayed in jail before trial, but wealthy defendants held on similar charges were able to pay for their freedom. The studies also showed that defendants who could not post bail were more likely to lose their cases. This supported the Supreme Court's statement in *Hudson v. Parker* (1895) that it was easier for a defendant to prepare a defense if he or she wasn't in jail. Adding to the unfairness, the data showed that defendants who belonged to a racial minority were less likely than white defendants to have bail set at an affordable amount.

Responding to these studies, Congress passed the Bail Reform Act of 1966. Under the act, most defendants were released from jail on their own recognizance (on their honor) without posting bail. Under the terms of the new law, a defendant could only be required to post bail if the court believed the defendant would otherwise flee.

However, the law allowed judges to impose numerous conditions on defendants who were released from jail without bail. Conditions included requiring a defendant to:

- remain crime-free before trial;
- stay within the court's jurisdiction (area of authority);

When too much isn't enough

Four months after the *Stack* decision, the Supreme Court heard another bail case—*Carlson v. Landon* (1952). In this case, four foreigners were charged with being members of the Communist Party. At this time, many political leaders in the United States believed that the

- avoid contact with victims or witnesses;

- comply with a curfew; and

- refrain (hold back) from using alcohol or drugs.

If a defendant failed to meet the court's conditions, he or she could be returned to jail to await trial. Nonetheless, the end result of the Bail Reform Act of 1966 was that many poor defendants were able to stay out of jail before their trials.

By the 1980s, public debate was focused less on the fairness of the bail system, and more on curbing crime. In 1984, reacting to the public perception that some defendants were committing crimes while waiting for trial, Congress enacted the Bail Reform Act of 1984. The new act changed the government's approach to bail by officially introducing the concept of preventive detention—that is, keeping defendants in jail to keep them from committing crimes. The Supreme Court decision in *Carlson v. Landon* (1952) had established that the government *could* retain defendants without bail if they posed a danger to the community. But Congress had never passed a law making such preventive detentions official government policy.

Under the Bail Reform Act of 1984, certain types of defendants could be held without bail in order to protect the public: defendants already convicted of a serious crime; defendants arrested while out on bail in a different case; and defendants arrested within five years of release from prison for a serious crime.

In order to refuse bail, a judge had to consider: the nature of the crime; whether the crime involved violence or drugs; how strong the evidence in the case was; the defendant's personal history; and the danger the defendant posed to the community. Some argued the Bail Reform Act violated the Excessive Bail Clause. However, in *United States v. Salerno* (1987), the Supreme Court ruled that the law was in fact constitutional.

Communist Party, an international political movement, was interested in overthrowing the U.S. government. Needless to say, the party had been outlawed.

The defendants were detained without bail. The government argued that releasing the defendants "would endanger the welfare and safety of the

United States." The defendants, however, argued that not setting bail in their case violated the Excessive Bail Clause. After all, the purpose of the Excessive Bail Clause was to keep bail reasonably affordable. What could be more excessive than not allowing a defendant to post bail at any price?

But the Supreme Court ruled that the Eighth Amendment did not ensure the right to bail in all cases. Indeed, defendants in capital cases had long been denied bail. What made the *Carlson* case different was the reason the government did not set bail. Previously, bail was denied to keep defendants from fleeing. In this case, the government denied bail because it felt the defendants posed a danger to society. The *Carlson* ruling gave the government greater leeway in deciding who could be denied bail.

Right to bail! What right to bail?

In 1987, the Supreme Court heard the case of *United States v. Salerno*. Salerno and Vincent Cafaro had been arrested and charged with racketeering (organized crime). At a hearing before their trial, Salerno and Cafaro were denied bail under the Bail Reform Act of 1984. The act allowed preventive detention (keeping a person in jail for safety reasons) of certain defendants (see "Retooling America's Bail System" box).

The defendants argued that the act violated the Excessive Bail Clause. The Supreme Court disagreed, and ruled again that nothing in the Eighth Amendment specifically guarantees bail in all cases. In its decision, the Court also stated that a primary concern of government was "the safety and indeed the lives of its citizens." Therefore, the Court could not object to the preventive detention of dangerous defendants in a "carefully limited" number of cases.

While Congress has repeatedly provided courts with guidelines for setting bail, the Supreme Court's various Excessive Bail decisions have yet to offer a hard and fast interpretation of what constitutes excessive bail.

Drawing the Line on Fines

The Excessive Fines Clause received very little attention from the U.S. Supreme Court until the late twentieth century when two separate rulings helped define the clause.

Some fines are dandy

In 1989, the Supreme Court heard the case of *Browning-Ferris Industries of Vermont, Inc. v. Kelco Disposal, Inc.* In that case, a jury had ordered Browning-Ferris to pay $6 million dollars in fines to one of its competitors, Kelco Disposal, Inc. Lawyers for Browning-Ferris argued that the huge sum violated the Excessive Fines Clause of the Eighth Amendment. However, the Supreme Court ruled that the Eighth Amendment only covered fines paid to the government, and did not apply to fines paid to private parties.

You can't take it with you

In *United States v. Bajakajian* (1998), Hosep Bajakajian pleaded guilty to attempting to leave the country with $357,144 without telling the government that he was taking the money. This violated a federal law that requires a person to declare (announce to authorities) any amount of cash over $10,000 dollars that he or she takes out of the United States. The government argued that Bajakajian and his wife should have to forfeit (give up) all of the cash they had been carrying. The trial court however, only fined the couple $15,000. The government took the case to the Supreme Court, but the Supreme Court ruled that forcing Bajakajian to give up all $357,144 would violate the Excessive Fines Clause.

Although the decision established that there could indeed exist such a thing as an excessive government fine, the case did not provide a set of guidelines for determining what makes a particular fine excessive.

Cruel and Unusual Punishment

Corporal punishment persisted in the United States after ratification of the U.S. Constitution and the Bill of Rights. But by the end of the eighteenth century, public opinion in the country had turned against physical punishments, and favored incarceration (prison).

The U.S. Supreme Court has consistently ruled that most corporal punishments are cruel and unusual. In *Wilkerson v. Utah* (1878), the Court ruled that disemboweling (cutting out inner organs) of a live person was cruel and unusual. In *in re Kemmler* (1890), the Court reaffirmed that "burning at the stake, crucifixion (nailing to a cross), [and] breaking on the wheel" were also unconstitutional. In *Skinner v. Oklahoma* (1942), the U.S. Supreme Court ruled that the physical sterilization (removal of sexual organs) of criminals was also unconstitutional.

OUCH! The Court has allowed government entities to continue one mild form of corporal punishment. In *Ingraham v. Wright* (1977), the Supreme Court ruled that the Eighth Amendment does *not* ban public schools from using physical punishment to discipline children.

CRUEL AND UNUSUAL PUNISHMENTS BEHIND BARS

One of the purposes of the Eighth Amendment was to prevent the U.S. government from inflicting the sorts of violent physical punishments that were still being used in England at the end of the eighteenth century. At that time in America, the practice of incarcerating (imprisoning) criminals had already begun to replace corporal punishment.

The first American prisons were generally clean, quiet places. Prisoners were expected to reflect on their crimes in silence while serving their sentences. Throughout the nineteenth century, public attitudes toward incarceration changed. Many prisons became filthy, dangerous places where the main purpose was simply to keep criminals off the streets.

The U.S. Supreme Court did not apply the Eighth Amendment to the issue of prison conditions until 1976, when it heard the case of *Estelle v. Gamble*. In that case, the Court ruled that the "deliberate indifference to serious medical needs of prisoners constitutes 'unnecessary and wanton infliction of pain,'" and therefore violates the Eighth Amendment.

A large number of the prison-related cruel and unusual punishment claims relate to alleged abuse at the hands of prison guards. In

Deadly Rulings: Applying the Eighth Amendment to Capital Punishment

The most common method of capital punishment in the colonies before the War was death by hanging. It remained so in the United States throughout the nineteenth century. In *Wilkerson v. Utah* (1878), the Supreme Court ruled that the public shooting of a convicted murderer was not cruel and unusual punishment.

However, the Court did look at punishments it considered excessive. The court said that " punishments of torture . . . and all others in the same line of unnecessary cruelty, are forbidden" by the Eighth Amendment. In the case of *In re Kemmler* (1890), the Court further stated that "[p]unishments are cruel when they involve torture or a lingering (drawn out) death."

Whitley v. Albers (1986), Gerald Albers, an inmate at the Oregon State Penitentiary, was shot in the leg during a prison riot. Albers claimed that the shooting constituted cruel and unusual punishment. But the Supreme Court ruled that Albers failed to prove that prison officials had acted unnecessarily or carelessly. Therefore, the shooting did not violate Albers Eighth Amendment rights.

However, in *Hudson v. McMillian* (1992), the Court ruled differently, even though a prisoner had not been hurt as badly as Albers had. Keith J. Hudson was a prisoner in a Louisiana state prison, and was beaten by two guards as their supervisor watched.

Hudson suffered bruises, loosened teeth, and swelling in his face, and claimed that the beating amounted to cruel and unusual punishment. Prison officials argued that the beatings could not be considered cruel and unusual punishment because Hudson's injuries were relatively minor. The Supreme Court disagreed. It ruled that a prisoner could bring a claim of excessive force under the Cruel and Unusual Punishments Clause, even if his or her injuries were minor and required no medical attention.

In general, the Court has ruled that prison officials who purposely or carelessly cause a prisoner physical or medical harm risk violating the Eighth Amendment Cruel and Unusual Punishment Clause.

Cruel or usual?

However, those rulings in no way stopped capital punishment. In 1998, thirty-two states authorized capital punishment. Legal methods of execution in the United States include hanging, shooting, gas chamber, lethal injection (death by a poisoned injection), and electrocution (death by electricity).

The most controversial of these methods of execution is the gas chamber. It is also the slowest to bring about death. During a gas chamber execution, the prisoner is placed in a closed cell that is quickly filled with poisonous fumes. The method is used by only three states: California, Maryland, and Arizona.

In *Gomez v. California* (1992), the Supreme Court refused to strike down California's use of the gas chamber. However, Justices John Paul Stevens and Harry A. Blackmun opposed the use of gas chambers. They called attention to the punishment's cruelty by citing one witness's description of Don Eugene Harding's execution in an Arizona gas chamber.

> **When the fumes enveloped Don's head he took a quick breath. A few seconds later he looked in my direction. His face was red and contorted as if he were attempting to fight through tremendous pain . . . [h]e was shuddering uncontrollably and his body was racked with spasms. His head continued to snap back . . . Don Harding took ten minutes and thirty-one seconds to die.**

The Court's refusal to outlaw the gas chamber shows how much the Court's opinion can change over time. It's hard to imagine that the justices who decided *In re Kemmler* in 1890 would not have ruled that the gas chamber execution described above did not involve "torture or a lingering death."

Killing the death penalty

The Supreme Court temporarily outlawed *all* forms of capital punishment in the 1970s. Throughout the nineteenth and early twentieth cen-

Execution by hanging is one of five legal methods of execution in the United States.

Reproduced by permission of Archive Photos, Inc.

tury, the Court had never questioned the states' right to impose the death penalty for capital crimes. It may be argued that no punishment is crueler than actually killing a defendant. However, it is much harder to argue that the death penalty is in any way unusual—governments have executed criminals throughout recorded history.

But in the 1950s and 1960s, legal professionals made thorough studies of how capital punishment was imposed. Like similar studies of the bail system in America, studies of the death penalty revealed an unfair system. African American defendants and poor defendants were more likely than white or wealthy defendants to be sentenced to death.

UNEQUAL PUNISHMENT IS CRUEL AND UNUSUAL. In 1972, the Supreme Court examined this issue in three cases: *Furman v. Georgia,* and two companion cases heard at the same time, *Jackson v. Georgia* and *Branch v. Texas.* After hearing evidence that showed patterns of discrimination in issuing death sentences, the justices voted five to four to put an end to the death penalty in the United States.

Two of the five justices who voted to end capital punishment argued that the death penalty itself was unconstitutional under the Eighth Amendment in all circumstances: Thurgood Marshall, and William H. Brennan. However, the other three justices found that the problem with capital punishment in the United States was not the punishment itself, but how courts decided who received such punishments.

Justice William O. Douglas looked at the data collected in several studies. He argued that because capital punishment discriminated against black defendants and poor defendants, it was "not compatible with the idea of equal protection of the laws that is implicit (suggested) in the ban on 'cruel and unusual' punishments." Justice Douglas said the Eighth Amendment required laws that were "evenhanded, nonselective, and nonarbitrary...."

Justice Byron R. White also argued that the problem with the death penalty was that it was imposed unfairly. As did Justice Potter Stewart. In his opinion, Justice Stewart wrote that the death penalty was "freakishly imposed," and was cruel and unusual punishment "in the same way that being struck by lightning" was cruel and unusual.

The decision in *Furman* outlawed the death penalty for several years, and saved over 600 people from execution in the United States. But because the decision did not rule that the death penalty is *always* cruel and unusual, it left the door open for the return of capital punishment under a more fair system.

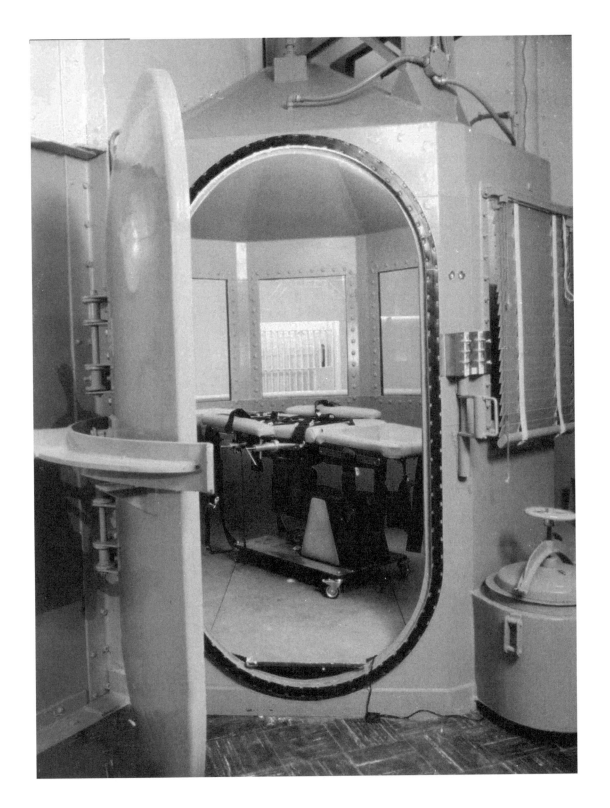

Capital punishment is resurrected

After the *Furman* decision, states revised their capital punishment laws, and addressed the unfairness that had been revealed in their systems. States changed their laws to give judges and juries more guidance in deciding whether or not to impose the death penalty. The statutes also gave defendants who were convicted of capital offenses the right to an automatic appeal (rehearing) of their case.

On July 2, 1976, the Supreme Court reinstated the death penalty with its decisions in three cases: *Gregg v. Georgia* (1976), *Proffitt v. Florida* (1976), and *Jurek v. Texas* (1976).

By a seven to two vote, the Court ruled that the states in those cases had cured the flaws in their capital punishment laws pointed out in *Furman.* The decision pointed the way for other states to legally bring back the death penalty.

An eye for an eye, or an eye for a tooth?

Since the drafting of the Eighth Amendment, fewer and fewer crimes have been classified as capital offenses. In *Enmund v. Florida* (1982), the Supreme Court officially limited the death penalty's uses to persons convicted of murder (intentional killing). The Court modified that decision in *Tison v. Arizona* (1987). The Court ruled that a person who commits a dangerous felony resulting in a death (even if the killing was unintentional) could also be executed.

Since the *Tison* decision, Congress has passed the Drug Kingpin Act (1988), and the Federal Death Penalty Act (1994). The Drug Kingpin Act made high-level drug trafficking (dealing) a capital offense. The Federal Death Penalty Act made approximately fifty crimes punishable by death, including several that do not involve murder of killing. To date, no one has been sentenced to execution under these laws, so the Supreme Court has not ruled on their constitutionality.

Making the Punishment Fit the Crime

The rulings in *Enmund v. Florida* and *Tison v. Arizona* raise the issue of proportional (similar in size or importance) punishment and the Eighth Amendment. The fundamental principle behind proportionality is that the punishment should fit the crime. A pickpocket should not face death, and someone who double-parks should not face prison.

Eigth Amendment

OPPOSITE PAGE:

The lethal injection chamber is similar to a small operating room, where the operating table has restraints to hold the prisoner in place while the deadly chemicals are being injected into their body. Reproduced by permission of AP/Wide World Photos.

**Eigth
Amendment**

The first important decision on proportionality came in the case of *Weems v. United States* (1910). In that case, Paul A. Weems was convicted of falsifying a public document. He was sentenced to hard labor for twelve to twenty years. Weems argued that the sentence was cruel and unusual, because the seriousness of the punishment was not proportionate to the seriousness of the crime.

After examining sentences in similar cases and sentences for more serious crimes, the Supreme Court agreed with Weems, and overruled the sentence. This was the first time that the Court specifically ruled that the

The electric chair is one of the more highly used methods of execution in the United States.

Reproduced by permission of the Corbis Corporation (Bellevue).

Cruel and Unusual Punishments Clause was designed, in part, to balance sentences (keep them proportionate) with the crime being punished.

In *Coker v. Georgia* (1977), the court ruled that the execution of a man for the rape of an adult woman was a "grossly disproportionate" punishment for the crime committed. But it was the case of *Solem v. Helm* (1983) in which the Court gave specific guidelines for deciding whether a punishment was proportional to the crime.

In that case, Jerry Buckley Helm was convicted of passing a bad check for one hundred dollars in South Dakota. Helm had a long history of nonviolent crime. He was sentenced to life in prison without the possibility of parole.

In a five to four vote, the Supreme Court ruled that the sentence was cruel and unusual, because it was disproportionate to the seriousness of the offense. In its decision, the Court ruled that courts must do three things to decide whether a sentence is proportional: compare the seriousness of the offense with the harshness of the penalty; compare the sentence with sentences for other crimes in the same jurisdiction (jurisdiction is a court's area of authority); and compare the sentence with sentences given out for the same crime in other courts' jurisdictions.

Who says punishment should be proportionate?

With the *Solem* ruling, the Supreme Court took for granted the Eight Amendment's proportional sentencing requirement. However, in *Harmelin v. Michigan* (1991), the Court seemed to forget this requirement. In *Harmelin,* a Michigan man was convicted of possessing over 650 grams of cocaine, and was sentenced to life in prison without the possibility of parole. The defendant argued that the punishment was cruel and unusual, and disproportionate to the crime.

When the case came before the Supreme Court, five justices ruled that the sentence was severe, but not necessarily disproportionate. The Court upheld the sentence. The four dissenting justices (those in disagreement with the majority) argued that the very "notion" that Harmelin's sentence was in any way proportional was "itself both cruel and unusual."

But more important than the justices disagreement over the proportionality of Harmelin's sentence was the opinion put forth by Justice Antonin Scalia and Chief Justice William H. Rehnquist. Justices Scalia and Rehnquist argued that it didn't matter whether Harmelin's punishment was disproportionate to his crime—the Eighth Amendment simply

Eigth Amendment

did not contain any requirement that every punishment somehow "fit" the crime.

All of the other justices argued that the Eighth Amendment required proportional punishments, but Justices Scalia and Rehnquist's opinions cast a shadow of doubt over the relationship between proportionality and the Eighth Amendment.

A Vague but Powerful Legacy

Some two hundred years after Patrick Henry and William Smith objected to the vague language of the Eighth Amendment, there is still little agreement on exactly what is meant by excessive bail, excessive fines, or cruel and unusual punishment. As vague as the amendment's clauses remain, the Eighth Amendment has nonetheless provided the Supreme Court with a means of regulating excessive bail and punishment.

While the Court has ruled in several cases that the government may legally deny bail to dangerous defendants, it has also repeatedly held that in most cases, defendants have the right to reasonable bail.

Aided by public sentiment, the Supreme Court has also used the Eighth Amendment to banish most corporal punishments from the legal system. The Supreme Court has consistently ruled that the ultimate punishment, death, *is* constitutional. However, it has used the Eighth Amendment to take steps against unfair sentencing procedures in capital punishment cases, and to outlaw most forms of execution that involve torture or lingering death.

Finally, there has been some disagreements among the justices. However, the Court has generally used the Eighth Amendment's prohibition against cruel and unusual punishment and excessive fines to require that crimes or offenses are proportionately punished.

Sources

Books

Berger, Raoul. "The Cruel and Unusual Punishments Clause." In *The Bill of Rights.* Edited by Eugene W. Hickok, Jr. Charlottesville: University Press of Virginia, 1991.

Encyclopedia of World Biography. 17 vols. Detroit, MI: Gale Research, 1998.

Hickok, Jr., Eugene W., ed. *The Bill of Rights: Original Meaning and Current Understanding.* Charlottesville, VA: University Press of Virginia, 1991.

West's Encyclopedia of American Law. 12 vols. St. Paul, MN: West Group, 1998.

Eigth
Amendment

Articles

Acosta, Sandra R. "Imposing the Death Penalty Upon Drug Kingpins." *Harvard Journal on Legislation* 27 (summer 1990): 596–602, 612.

Beale, Sara Sun, and Paul H. Haagen. "Review of *The Hanging Tree: Execution and the English People, 1770–1868* by V.A.C. Gatrell." *Michigan Law Review Association* 94 (1996): 1622–25.

Boston, Gerald W. "Punitive Damages and the Eighth Amendment: Application of the Excessive Fines Clause." *Cooley Law Review* 5 (Michaelmas Term 1988): 667, 703–4.

Bukowski, Jeffrey D. "The Eighth Amendment and Original Intent: Applying the Prohibition Against Cruel and Unusual Punishments to Prison Deprivation Cases Is Not Beyond the Bounds of History and Precedent." *Dickinson Law Review* 99 (winter 1995): 419–28, 436–37.

Bund, Jennifer. "Did You Say Chemical Castration?" *University of Pittsburgh Law Review* 59 (fall 1997): 157–65.

Caminker, Evan, and Erwin Chemerinsky. "The Lawless Execution of Robert Alton Harris." *Yale Law Journal* 102 (October 1992): 225–28.

Cordray, Margaret Meriwether. "Contempt Sanctions and the Excessive Fines Clause." *North Carolina Law Review* 76 (January 1998): 407, 419–28, 462.

Garvey, Stephen P. "Freeing Prisoners' Labor." *Stanford Law Review* 50 (January 1998) 339, 345–65.

Genty, Philip M. "Confusing Punishment with Custodial Care: The Troublesome Legacy of Estelle v. Gamble." *Vermont Law Review* 21 (1997): 379.

Gorman, Tessa M. "Back On the Chain Gang: Why the Eighth Amendment and the History of Slavery Proscribe the Resurgence of Chain Gangs." *California Law Review* 85 (March 1997): 441–43.

McCord, David, "Imagining a Retributivist Alternative to Capital Punishment." *Florida Law Review* 50 (January 1998): 1, 83–88, 143.

Metzmeier, Kurt X. "Preventive Detention: A Comparison of Bail Refusal Practices in the United States, England, Canada and Other Common Law Nations." *Pace International Law Review* 8 (spring 1996): 399–413, 434.

Robertson, James E. "Houses of the Dead: Warehouse Prisons, Paradigm Change, and the Supreme Court." *Houston Law Review* 34 (winter 1997): 1003–25, 1062–63.

Robinson, Peyton, "Judge Over Jury: Judicial Discretion in the Federal Death Penalty Under the Drug Kingpin Act." *University of Kansas Law Review* 45 (August 1997): 1491–94.

Snyder, Brad. "Disparate Impact on Death Row: M.L.B. and the Indigent's Right to Counsel at Capital State Postconviction Proceedings." *Yale Law Journal* 107 (May 1998): 2211, 2213.

Verrilli, Donald B., Jr. "The Eighth Amendment and the Right to Bail: Historical Perspectives." *Columbia Law Review* 82 (March 1982): 328–62.

Yeargin, D. Grayson. "Review Proceedings." *Georgetown Law Journal* 86 (June 1998): 1884, 1891–93.

Constitution of the
United States of America

We the People of the United States, in Order to form a more perfect Union, establish Justice, insure domestic Tranquility, provide for the common defense, promote the general Welfare, and secure the Blessings of Liberty to ourselves and our Posterity, do ordain and establish this Constitution for the United States of America.

Article I

Items in italic have since been amended or superseded.
A portion of Article I, Section 2, was modified by Section 2 of the Fourteenth Amendment; Article I, Section 3, was modified by the Seventeenth Amendment; Article I, Section 4, was modified by Section 2 of the Twentieth Amendment; and Article I, Section 9, was modified by the Sixteenth Amendment.

Section 1.

All legislative Powers herein granted shall be vested in a Congress of the United States, which shall consist of a Senate and House of Representatives.

Section 2.

The House of Representatives shall be composed of Members chosen every second Year by the People of the several States, and the Electors in each State shall have the Qualifications requisite for Electors of the most numerous Branch of the State Legislature.

No Person shall be a Representative who shall not have attained to the Age of twenty five Years, and been seven Years a Citizen of the

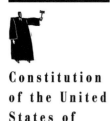

Constitution of the United States of America

United States, and who shall not, when elected, be an Inhabitant of that State in which he shall be chosen.

Representatives and direct Taxes shall be apportioned among the several States which may be included within this Union, according to their respective Numbers, which shall be determined by adding to the whole Number of free Persons, including those bound to Service for a Term of Years, and excluding Indians not taxed, three fifths of all other Persons. The actual Enumeration shall be made within three Years after the first Meeting of the Congress of the United States, and within every subsequent Term of ten Years, in such Manner as they shall by Law direct. The Number of Representatives shall not exceed one for every thirty Thousand, but each State shall have at Least one Representative; and until such enumeration shall be made, the State of New Hampshire shall be entitled to chuse three, Massachusetts eight, Rhode-Island and Providence Plantations one, Connecticut five, New-York six, New Jersey four, Pennsylvania eight, Delaware one, Maryland six, Virginia ten, North Carolina five, South Carolina five, and Georgia three.

When vacancies happen in the Representation from any State, the Executive Authority thereof shall issue Writs of Election to fill such Vacancies.

The House of Representatives shall chuse their Speaker and other Officers; and shall have the sole Power of Impeachment.

Section 3.

The Senate of the United States shall be composed of two Senators from each State, *chosen by the Legislature thereof* for six Years; and each Senator shall have one Vote.

Immediately after they shall be assembled in Consequence of the first Election, they shall be divided as equally as may be into three Classes. The Seats of the Senators of the first Class shall be vacated at the Expiration of the second Year, of the second Class at the Expiration of the fourth Year, and of the third Class at the Expiration of the sixth Year, so that one third may be chosen every second Year; *and if Vacancies happen by Resignation, or otherwise, during the Recess of the Legislature of any State, the Executive thereof may make temporary Appointments until the next Meeting of the Legislature, which shall then fill such Vacancies.*

No Person shall be a Senator who shall not have attained to the Age of thirty Years, and been nine Years a Citizen of the United States, and who shall not, when elected, be an Inhabitant of that State for which he shall be chosen.

The Vice President of the United States shall be President of the Senate, but shall have no Vote, unless they be equally divided.

The Senate shall chuse their other Officers, and also a President pro tempore, in the Absence of the Vice President, or when he shall exercise the Office of President of the United States.

The Senate shall have the sole Power to try all Impeachments. When sitting for that Purpose, they shall be on Oath or Affirmation. When the President of the United States is tried, the Chief Justice shall preside: And no Person shall be convicted without the Concurrence of two thirds of the Members present.

Judgment in Cases of Impeachment shall not extend further than to removal from Office, and disqualification to hold and enjoy any Office of honor, Trust or Profit under the United States: but the Party convicted shall nevertheless be liable and subject to Indictment, Trial, Judgment and Punishment, according to Law.

Section 4.

The Times, Places and Manner of holding Elections for Senators and Representatives, shall be prescribed in each State by the Legislature thereof; but the Congress may at any time by Law make or alter such Regulations, except as to the Places of chusing Senators.

The Congress shall assemble at least once in every Year, and such Meeting shall *be on the first Monday in December,* unless they shall by Law appoint a different Day.

Section 5.

Each House shall be the Judge of the Elections, Returns and Qualifications of its own Members, and a Majority of each shall constitute a Quorum to do Business; but a smaller Number may adjourn from day to day, and may be authorized to compel the Attendance of absent Members, in such Manner, and under such Penalties as each House may provide.

Each House may determine the Rules of its Proceedings, punish its Members for disorderly Behaviour, and, with the Concurrence of two thirds, expel a Member.

Each House shall keep a Journal of its Proceedings, and from time to time publish the same, excepting such Parts as may in their Judgment

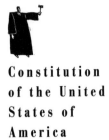
require Secrecy; and the Yeas and Nays of the Members of either House on any question shall, at the Desire of one fifth of those Present, be entered on the Journal.

Neither House, during the Session of Congress, shall, without the Consent of the other, adjourn for more than three days, nor to any other Place than that in which the two Houses shall be sitting.

Section 6.

The Senators and Representatives shall receive a Compensation for their Services, to be ascertained by Law, and paid out of the Treasury of the United States. They shall in all Cases, except Treason, Felony and Breach of the Peace, be privileged from Arrest during their Attendance at the Session of their respective Houses, and in going to and returning from the same; and for any Speech or Debate in either House, they shall not be questioned in any other Place.

No Senator or Representative shall, during the Time for which he was elected, be appointed to any civil Office under the Authority of the United States, which shall have been created, or the Emoluments where-of shall have been encreased during such time; and no Person holding any Office under the United States, shall be a Member of either House during his Continuance in Office.

Section 7.

All Bills for raising Revenue shall originate in the House of Representatives; but the Senate may propose or concur with Amendments as on other Bills.

Every Bill which shall have passed the House of Representatives and the Senate, shall, before it become a Law, be presented to the President of the United States: If he approve he shall sign it, but if not he shall return it, with his Objections to that House in which it shall have originated, who shall enter the Objections at large on their Journal, and proceed to reconsider it. If after such Reconsideration two thirds of that House shall agree to pass the Bill, it shall be sent, together with the Objections, to the other House, by which it shall likewise be reconsidered, and if approved by two thirds of that House, it shall become a Law. But in all such Cases the Votes of both Houses shall be determined by yeas and Nays, and the Names of the Persons voting for and against the Bill shall be entered on the Journal of each House respectively. If any Bill shall not be returned by the President within ten Days (Sundays excepted) after it shall have been presented to him, the Same shall be a Law, in like Manner as if he had signed it, unless the Congress by their Adjournment prevent its Return, in which Case it shall not be a Law.

Every Order, Resolution, or Vote to which the Concurrence of the Senate and House of Representatives may be necessary (except on a question of Adjournment) shall be presented to the President of the United States; and before the Same shall take Effect, shall be approved by him, or being disapproved by him, shall be repassed by two thirds of the Senate and House of Representatives, according to the Rules and Limitations prescribed in the Case of a Bill.

Constitution of the United States of America

Section 8.

The Congress shall have Power To lay and collect Taxes, Duties, Imposts and Excises, to pay the Debts and provide for the common Defence and general Welfare of the United States; but all Duties, Imposts and Excises shall be uniform throughout the United States;

To borrow Money on the credit of the United States;

To regulate Commerce with foreign Nations, and among the several States, and with the Indian Tribes;

To establish an uniform Rule of Naturalization, and uniform Laws on the subject of Bankruptcies throughout the United States;

To coin Money, regulate the Value thereof, and of foreign Coin, and fix the Standard of Weights and Measures;

To provide for the Punishment of counterfeiting the Securities and current Coin of the United States;

To establish Post Offices and post Roads;

To promote the Progress of Science and useful Arts, by securing for limited Times to Authors and Inventors the exclusive Right to their respective Writings and Discoveries;

To constitute Tribunals inferior to the supreme Court;

To define and punish Piracies and Felonies committed on the high Seas, and Offences against the Law of Nations;

To declare War, grant Letters of Marque and Reprisal, and make Rules concerning Captures on Land and Water;

To raise and support Armies, but no Appropriation of Money to that Use shall be for a longer Term than two Years;

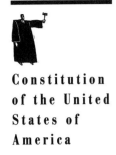

To provide and maintain a Navy;

To make Rules for the Government and Regulation of the land and naval Forces;

To provide for calling forth the Militia to execute the Laws of the Union, suppress Insurrections and repel Invasions;

To provide for organizing, arming, and disciplining, the Militia, and for governing such Part of them as may be employed in the Service of the United States, reserving to the States respectively, the Appointment of the Officers, and the Authority of training the Militia according to the discipline prescribed by Congress;

To exercise exclusive Legislation in all Cases whatsoever, over such District (not exceeding ten Miles square) as may, by Cession of particular States, and the Acceptance of Congress, become the Seat of the Government of the United States, and to exercise like Authority over all Places purchased by the Consent of the Legislature of the State in which the Same shall be, for the Erection of Forts, Magazines, Arsenals, dock-Yards, and other needful Buildings;—And

To make all Laws which shall be necessary and proper for carrying into Execution the foregoing Powers, and all other Powers vested by this Constitution in the Government of the United States, or in any Department or Officer thereof.

Section 9.

The Migration or Importation of such Persons as any of the States now existing shall think proper to admit, shall not be prohibited by the Congress prior to the Year one thousand eight hundred and eight, but a Tax or duty may be imposed on such Importation, not exceeding ten dollars for each Person.

The Privilege of the Writ of Habeas Corpus shall not be suspended, unless when in Cases of Rebellion or Invasion the public Safety may require it.

No Bill of Attainder or ex post facto Law shall be passed.

No Capitation, or other direct, Tax shall be laid, *unless in Proportion to the Census or enumeration herein before directed to be taken.*

No Tax or Duty shall be laid on Articles exported from any State.

No Preference shall be given by any Regulation of Commerce or Revenue to the Ports of one State over those of another; nor shall

Vessels bound to, or from, one State, be obliged to enter, clear, or pay Duties in another.

No Money shall be drawn from the Treasury, but in Consequence of Appropriations made by Law; and a regular Statement and Account of the Receipts and Expenditures of all public Money shall be published from time to time.

No Title of Nobility shall be granted by the United States: And no Person holding any Office of Profit or Trust under them, shall, without the Consent of the Congress, accept of any present, Emolument, Office, or Title, of any kind whatever, from any King, Prince, or foreign State.

Section 10.

No State shall enter into any Treaty, Alliance, or Confederation; grant Letters of Marque and Reprisal; coin Money; emit Bills of Credit; make any Thing but gold and silver Coin a Tender in Payment of Debts; pass any Bill of Attainder, ex post facto Law, or Law impairing the Obligation of Contracts, or grant any Title of Nobility.

No State shall, without the Consent of the Congress, lay any Imposts or Duties on Imports or Exports, except what may be absolutely necessary for executing it's inspection Laws: and the net Produce of all Duties and Imposts, laid by any State on Imports or Exports, shall be for the Use of the Treasury of the United States; and all such Laws shall be subject to the Revision and Controul of the Congress.

No State shall, without the Consent of Congress, lay any Duty of Tonnage, keep Troops, or Ships of War in time of Peace, enter into any Agreement or Compact with another State, or with a foreign Power, or engage in War, unless actually invaded, or in such imminent Danger as will not admit of delay.

Article II

Article II, Section 1, was superseded by the Twelfth Amendment
Article II, Section 1, was modified by the Twenty-fifth Amendment.

Section 1.

The executive Power shall be vested in a President of the United States of America. He shall hold his Office during the Term of four Years, and, together with the Vice President, chosen for the same Term, be elected, as follows:

Constitution of the United States of America

Each State shall appoint, in such Manner as the Legislature thereof may direct, a Number of Electors, equal to the whole Number of Senators and Representatives to which the State may be entitled in the Congress: but no Senator or Representative, or Person holding an Office of Trust or Profit under the United States, shall be appointed an Elector.

The Electors shall meet in their respective States, and vote by Ballot for two Persons, of whom one at least shall not be an Inhabitant of the same State with themselves. And they shall make a List of all the Persons voted for, and of the Number of Votes for each; which List they shall sign and certify, and transmit sealed to the Seat of the Government of the United States, directed to the President of the Senate. The President of the Senate shall, in the Presence of the Senate and House of Representatives, open all the Certificates, and the Votes shall then be counted. The Person having the greatest Number of Votes shall be the President, if such Number be a Majority of the whole Number of Electors appointed; and if there be more than one who have such Majority, and have an equal Number of Votes, then the House of Representatives shall immediately chuse by Ballot one of them for President; and if no Person have a Majority, then from the five highest on the List the said House shall in like Manner chuse the President. But in chusing the President, the Votes shall be taken by States, the Representation from each State having one Vote; A quorum for this purpose shall consist of a Member or Members from two thirds of the States, and a Majority of all the States shall be necessary to a Choice. In every Case, after the Choice of the President, the Person having the greatest Number of Votes of the Electors shall be the Vice President. But if there should remain two or more who have equal Votes, the Senate shall chuse from them by Ballot the Vice President.

The Congress may determine the Time of chusing the Electors, and the Day on which they shall give their Votes; which Day shall be the same throughout the United States.

No Person except a natural born Citizen, or a Citizen of the United States, at the time of the Adoption of this Constitution, shall be eligible to the Office of President; neither shall any Person be eligible to that Office who shall not have attained to the Age of thirty five Years, and been fourteen Years a Resident within the United States.

In Case of the Removal of the President from Office, or of his Death, Resignation, or Inability to discharge the Powers and Duties of the said Office, the Same shall devolve on the Vice President, and the Congress may by Law provide for the Case of Removal, Death, Resignation or

Inability, both of the President and Vice President, declaring what Officer shall then act as President, and such Officer shall act accordingly, until the Disability be removed, or a President shall be elected.

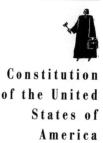

The President shall, at stated Times, receive for his Services, a Compensation, which shall neither be increased nor diminished during the Period for which he shall have been elected, and he shall not receive within that Period any other Emolument from the United States, or any of them.

Before he enter on the Execution of his Office, he shall take the following Oath or Affirmation:—"I do solemnly swear (or affirm) that I will faithfully execute the Office of President of the United States, and will to the best of my Ability, preserve, protect and defend the Constitution of the United States."

Section 2.

The President shall be Commander in Chief of the Army and Navy of the United States, and of the Militia of the several States, when called into the actual Service of the United States; he may require the Opinion, in writing, of the principal Officer in each of the executive Departments, upon any Subject relating to the Duties of their respective Offices, and he shall have Power to grant Reprieves and Pardons for Offences against the United States, except in Cases of Impeachment. He shall have Power, by and with the Advice and Consent of the Senate, to make Treaties, provided two thirds of the Senators present concur; and he shall nominate, and by and with the Advice and Consent of the Senate, shall appoint Ambassadors, other public Ministers and Consuls, Judges of the supreme Court, and all other Officers of the United States, whose Appointments are not herein otherwise provided for, and which shall be established by Law: but the Congress may by Law vest the Appointment of such inferior Officers, as they think proper, in the President alone, in the Courts of Law, or in the Heads of Departments.

The President shall have Power to fill up all Vacancies that may happen during the Recess of the Senate, by granting Commissions which shall expire at the End of their next Session.

Section 3.

He shall from time to time give to the Congress Information of the State of the Union, and recommend to their Consideration such Measures as he shall judge necessary and expedient; he may, on extraordinary

Constitution of the United States of America

Occasions, convene both Houses, or either of them, and in Case of Disagreement between them, with Respect to the Time of Adjournment, he may adjourn them to such Time as he shall think proper; he shall receive Ambassadors and other public Ministers; he shall take Care that the Laws be faithfully executed, and shall Commission all the Officers of the United States.

Section 4.

The President, Vice President and all civil Officers of the United States, shall be removed from Office on Impeachment for, and Conviction of, Treason, Bribery, or other high Crimes and Misdemeanors.

Article III

A portion of Section 2 was modified by the Eleventh Amendment.

Section 1.

The judicial Power of the United States shall be vested in one supreme Court, and in such inferior Courts as the Congress may from time to time ordain and establish. The Judges, both of the supreme and inferior Courts, shall hold their Offices during good Behaviour, and shall, at stated Times, receive for their Services a Compensation, which shall not be diminished during their Continuance in Office.

Section 2.

The judicial Power shall extend to all Cases, in Law and Equity, arising under this Constitution, the Laws of the United States, and Treaties made, or which shall be made, under their Authority;—to all Cases affecting Ambassadors, other public Ministers and Consuls;—to all Cases of admiralty and maritime Jurisdiction;—to Controversies to which the United States shall be a Party; to Controversies between two or more States;—*between a State and Citizens of another State;*—between Citizens of different States; between Citizens of the same State claiming Lands under Grants of different States, and between a State, or the Citizens thereof, and foreign States, Citizens or Subjects.

In all Cases affecting Ambassadors, other public Ministers and Consuls, and those in which a State shall be Party, the supreme Court shall have original Jurisdiction. In all the other Cases before mentioned, the supreme Court shall have appellate Jurisdiction, both as to Law and

Fact, with such Exceptions, and under such Regulations as the Congress shall make.

The Trial of all Crimes, except in Cases of Impeachment, shall be by Jury; and such Trial shall be held in the State where the said Crimes shall have been committed; but when not committed within any State, the Trial shall be at such Place or Places as the Congress may by Law have directed.

Section 3.

Treason against the United States, shall consist only in levying War against them, or in adhering to their Enemies, giving them Aid and Comfort. No Person shall be convicted of Treason unless on the Testimony of two Witnesses to the same overt Act, or on Confession in open Court.

The Congress shall have Power to declare the Punishment of Treason, but no Attainder of Treason shall work Corruption of Blood, or Forfeiture except during the Life of the Person attainted.

Article IV

A portion of Section 2 was superseded by the Thirteenth Amendment.

Section 1.

Full Faith and Credit shall be given in each State to the public Acts, Records, and judicial Proceedings of every other State. And the Congress may by general Laws prescribe the Manner in which such Acts, Records and Proceedings shall be proved, and the Effect thereof.

Section 2.

The Citizens of each State shall be entitled to all Privileges and Immunities of Citizens in the several States.

A Person charged in any State with Treason, Felony, or other Crime, who shall flee from Justice, and be found in another State, shall on Demand of the executive Authority of the State from which he fled, be delivered up, to be removed to the State having Jurisdiction of the Crime.

No Person held to Service or Labour in one State, under the Laws thereof, escaping into another, shall, in Consequence of any Law or Regulation therein, be discharged from such Service or Labour, but shall be delivered up on Claim of the Party to whom such Service or Labour may be due.

Constitution
of the United
States of
America

Section 3.

New States may be admitted by the Congress into this Union; but no new State shall be formed or erected within the Jurisdiction of any other State; nor any State be formed by the Junction of two or more States, or Parts of States, without the Consent of the Legislatures of the States concerned as well as of the Congress.

The Congress shall have Power to dispose of and make all needful Rules and Regulations respecting the Territory or other Property belonging to the United States; and nothing in this Constitution shall be so construed as to Prejudice any Claims of the United States, or of any particular State.

Section 4.

The United States shall guarantee to every State in this Union a Republican Form of Government, and shall protect each of them against Invasion; and on Application of the Legislature, or of the Executive (when the Legislature cannot be convened), against domestic Violence.

Article V

The Congress, whenever two thirds of both Houses shall deem it necessary, shall propose Amendments to this Constitution, or, on the Application of the Legislatures of two thirds of the several States, shall call a Convention for proposing Amendments, which, in either Case, shall be valid to all Intents and Purposes, as Part of this Constitution, when ratified by the Legislatures of three fourths of the several States, or by Conventions in three fourths thereof, as the one or the other Mode of Ratification may be proposed by the Congress; Provided that no Amendment which may be made prior to the Year One thousand eight hundred and eight shall in any Manner affect the first and fourth Clauses in the Ninth Section of the first Article; and that no State, without its Consent, shall be deprived of its equal Suffrage in the Senate.

Article VI

All Debts contracted and Engagements entered into, before the Adoption of this Constitution, shall be as valid against the United States under this Constitution, as under the Confederation.

This Constitution, and the Laws of the United States which shall be made in Pursuance thereof; and all Treaties made, or which shall be made, under the Authority of the United States, shall be the supreme Law of the Land; and the Judges in every State shall be bound thereby, any Thing in the Constitution or Laws of any State to the Contrary notwithstanding.

The Senators and Representatives before mentioned, and the Members of the several State Legislatures, and all executive and judicial Officers, both of the United States and of the several States, shall be bound by Oath or Affirmation, to support this Constitution; but no religious Test shall ever be required as a Qualification to any Office or public Trust under the United States.

Article VII

The Ratification of the Conventions of nine States, shall be sufficient for the Establishment of this Constitution between the States so ratifying the Same.

Attest William Jackson Secretary

Done in Convention by the Unanimous Consent of the States present the Seventeenth Day of September in the Year of our Lord one thousand seven hundred and Eighty seven and of the Independence of the United States of America the Twelfth In witness whereof We have hereunto subscribed our Names,

G° Washington Presidt and deputy from Virginia

Delaware: Geo: Read, Gunning Bedford jun, John Dickinson, Richard Bassett, Jaco: Broom

Maryland: James McHenry, Dan of St Thos. Jenifer, Danl. Carroll

Virginia: John Blair—, James Madison Jr.

North Carolina: Wm. Blount, Richd. Dobbs Spaight, Hu Williamson

South Carolina: J. Rutledge, Charles Cotesworth Pinckney, Charles Pinckney, Pierce Butler

Georgia: William Few, Abr Baldwin

New Hampshire: John Langdon, Nicholas Gilman

Massachusetts: Nathaniel Gorham, Rufus King

Connecticut: Wm. Saml. Johnson Roger Sherman

New York: Alexander Hamilton

Constitution of the United States of America

New Jersey: Wil: Livingston, David Brearley, Wm. Paterson, Jona: Dayton

Pennsylvania: B Franklin, Thomas Mifflin, Robt. Morris, Geo. Clymer, Thos. FitzSimons, Jared Ingersoll, James Wilson, Gouv Morris

Index

A

Abington School District v. Schempp (1963), 1:7

abortion legislation. *See* amendment proposals and *Roe v. Wade*

Adair v. United States (1908), 1:111

Adams, John, 1:13, 57, 2:224–26, 2:237 (illus.), 2:237–39, 242, 244, 3:393, 438, 466

Adams, John Quincy, 2:243–44, 341

Adams, Samuel, 1:58

Adams v. New York (1904), 1:81–2

Adderly v. Florida (1966), 1:27

Afroyim v. Rusk (1967), 2:278

Age Discrimination in Employment Act of 1967 (ADEA), 1:152

Agostini v. Felton (1997), 1:9

Aguilar v. Felton (1985), 1:9

Aguilar v. Texas (1964), 1:77

Alien and Sedition Acts of 1798, 1:13

Allgeyer v. Louisiana (1897), 1:111, 2:281

amendment proposals, 3:508–28

abortion, 3:521, 525, 3:525 (illus.)

balanced budget proposal, 3:514–15, 521

child labor proposal, 3:513–17, 3:513 (illus.), 3:521

congressional term limits, 3:521, 525–26

District of Columbia statehood, 3:447, 522–23

Electoral College reform, 3:521–24

Equal Rights Amendment (ERA), 3:383, 517–21, 3:517 (illus.)

flag desecration, 3:521, 524

nobility proposal, 3:509–11, 3:510 (illus.)

American Medical Association (AMA), 2:189

American Woman Suffrage Association (AWSA), 3:373–74, 376

Anthony, Susan B., 3:373 (illus.), 3:373, 375, 378, 382

Anti–Saloon League, 3:360, 362, 402

Apodaca v. Oregon (1972), 1:127

Apportionment Clause, The, 2:274, 296–97, 298

Arizona v. Evans (1995), 1:86

Arthur, Chester A., 3:468–69

Articles of Confederation, 1:3, 34, 61–2, 74, 92, 121, 145, 162–63, 2:182, 184, 198, 205, 223, 276, 338, 3:422, 437, 498

Ashcraft v. Tennessee, (1944), 1:105

Ashwander v. Tennessee Valley Authority (1936), 2:186

Association Against the Prohibition Amendment (AAPA), 3:409, 412–13

Atlas Roofing Co. v. Occupational Safety & Health Review Commission (1977), 1:155

Attucks, Crispus, 1:58–9, 1:57 (illus.)

Index

Index

Index

H

I

J

Index

Index

I n d e x